T0131631

Dreams, Rainbows and Butterflies

ADRIAN. S. JONES

BALBOA.
PRESS

A DIVISION OF HAY HOUSE

Balboa Press books may be ordered through booksellers or by contacting:

Balboa Press
A Division of Hay House
1663 Liberty Drive
Bloomington, IN 47403
www.balboapress.com
1 (877) 407-4847

Because of the dynamic nature of the Internet, any web addresses or links contained in this book may have changed since publication and may no longer be valid. The views expressed in this work are solely those of the author and do not necessarily reflect the views of the publisher, and the publisher hereby disclaims any responsibility for them.

The author of this book does not dispense medical advice or prescribe the use of any technique as a form of treatment for physical, emotional, or medical problems without the advice of a physician, either directly or indirectly. The intent of the author is only to offer information of a general nature to help you in your quest for emotional and spiritual well-being. In the event you use any of the information in this book for yourself, which is your constitutional right, the author and the publisher assume no responsibility for your actions.

Any people depicted in stock imagery provided by Thinkstock are models, and such images are being used for illustrative purposes only. Certain stock imagery © Thinkstock.

Print information available on the last page.

ISBN: 978-1-5043-4060-1 (sc)
ISBN: 978-1-5043-4062-5 (hc)
ISBN: 978-1-5043-4061-8 (e)

Library of Congress Control Number: 2015915508

Balboa Press rev. date: 10/29/2015

For Our Children

Life is a journey of beautiful coincidence for your enjoyment and appreciation of love in a moment forever.

Always three kisses,

Always of love

x x x

Loving in Memory Forever a Moment

'I am not who but how and when,
I am not tell but show and do,
I am not life or death,
I am your teacher,
I am love.'

Carole Jones
X

1969–2011

Released of Heart to Fly on
the Wings of
Love

x

CONTENTS

A Second Chance

I woke abruptly from a deep sleep. My head was heavy and it hurt. I'd bolted upright too quickly, and for a split second the pain was unbearable. All I could see were fuzzy dots as the first complaining eye squinted open.

In the darkness, my attention was drawn immediately to the voice of a child whose small frame was silhouetted in the doorway. He spoke softly and with purpose. My son had awoken earlier than usual to answer the call of nature. He'd followed his usual routine of tiptoeing the short distance across the landing to the bathroom. A few minutes later, on his way back to bed, he heard an unfamiliar sound and decided to investigate. He opened the door and realised that something was not right. Sensing urgency, he whispered, 'Dad, Dad, I think there's something wrong with Mum.'

I turned and saw that he was right. Mummy was unconscious and gargling blood. She was unresponsive, and her white eyes were fixed, zombielike. She had bitten through her tongue, which bled badly from a large rip. Blood and foaming saliva semi-clogged her airway to the extent that red and white fluids seeped without interruption from her open mouth down the right side of her contorted face. The pillow upon which she rested as dead weight was stained with large

1

red and pink patches. She was shaking violently, gasping for breath and expelling a loud groaning moan.

Carole was in bad shape. Where to start? What to do? Many thoughts rushed through my head. My temples were cold, and an icy chill descended my spine. I needed professional help. I needed it urgently. I loosened the quilt that cocooned Carole and found her whole body rigid in a state of terrible trauma. I shouted loudly to Carole and stroked her face. There was no response. I squeezed her hand and then the other, and then I squeezed much tighter. No response.

As I reached for the phone, I realised that my son was still standing in the doorway. Calmly, I asked him to go and wake up his sister while I dialled the emergency services. Seconds later, two very anxious children were on the landing comforting each other and observing all manner of things. My immediate instinct was to protect them.

'I need your help, guys,' I said. 'Mummy's sick. I need you to go downstairs, put on all the lights and the TV, and open the front door. Look out for an ambulance.' As I glanced at them over my left shoulder, their faces spoke a thousand words. 'Now please, lights, TV, ambulance – off you go.'

I'd sent them to the relative safety of the lounge together. They were out of harm's way for the time being. What had they seen? Two or three minutes had passed since I'd exited sleep. Carole was still unconscious, still bleeding and foaming at the mouth. Her pupils were still rolled toward the back of their sockets. How long had she been like this? I had no idea what she was experiencing, but everything was telling me that her life was in danger.

For the first time, a very real sense of fear took hold. My heart raced. I struggled to stop it from breaking just long enough to control the emotional quaver in my throat. I fought with everything I had in that moment to stop the flow of tears which escaped silently down my face. The questions from a gentle voice on the other end of the phone helped me to stay focused as we monitored Carole's status together.

There was no change in her unconsciousness. With the phone lodged uncomfortably between my left ear and shoulder, I sat astride Carole in a position that did not restrict her movement. I'd already grabbed her tongue to unblock her airway. I held it with my left hand over the one-and-a-half-centimetre rip in an attempt to stop the bleeding. Her tongue was limp, salivary, and fleshy, and its natural movement was toward the back of her throat with each desperate inhalation. I was terrified that she would swallow it. With the first two fingers of my other hand, I cleared her airway as best I could.

I was covered in Carole's blood. I wiped my hands on my white cotton T-shirt, trying anxiously to maintain the continuity of her airway and control blood loss. Frantically I swapped hands, trying to keep her tongue in constant restraint. It just kept slipping through my fingers. Whenever I could, I stroked the side of her face gently so that she might know I was there. I talked emotionally to the woman of my dreams, telling her to fight, telling her that this was not her time. Carole continued to expel horrible sounds, as if trying to communicate with me through her unconsciousness. It was impossible to put her in the recovery position because she was rigid as her body shook violently.

I began to sweat and tried hard not to panic. Adrenaline shot through my body. The icy shiver returned and penetrated my core once more. My hands had started to shake, and my palms had become sticky. I talked to Carole, to my children who were still in the lounge, and to the voice on the phone. I whispered to God. It was difficult to retain focus, but I had to stay with Carole, and I willed her to stay with me until help arrived. I was fighting to hold it together. I had to. I had no choice. My eyes wanted to stream again, but I held the tears at bay temporarily and let my heart bleed silently instead. It broke in those moments into a million jagged pieces which tore at every fibre of my being. I had to keep going. Carole had to keep fighting.

In my moments of heart bleed, Carole and I did what we had always done. We were doing the things that defined our friendship. Somehow, we worked together to hang on to life for all it was worth. We loved life and had lived a life of love. We loved each other. We loved our children. We dug in deep that morning. I wasn't prepared to lose my best friend, and thoughts of Carole and our kids kept me going. It felt like Carole was hanging on by the slimmest of margins. Even though she remained unresponsive, I continued to talk to her and had to believe that she could hear me and that we would be OK. She was a fighter, and everything I sensed was telling me that she was fighting with all her might.

They say that your life flashes in front of you in extreme circumstances when danger threatens the very fabric of your existence. I can tell you that it did that morning – silently and in full colour, like a badly edited movie on extreme fast forward. Chronology and event connections were absent as my brain was flooded with a cinematic extravaganza that made terrible and inappropriately timed viewing.

We were flying a kite with the children ... our first lingering kiss ... the first dance on our special day ... holding hands in the rain. Carole was sleeping on the sofa, wrapping presents, feeding ducks, making angels in the snow. We were star-gazing by moonlight, driving through a meadow, blowing bubbles in the summer breeze, running breathlessly, and leaving hospital with our new-born. Sparks of pure white light appeared intermittently in my peripheral vision like the final flicker of a Roman candle. A sensation of floating washed over me from head to toe before the feeling of free fall seized my anxious mind. The sound of Carole's laughter, excited children at play, the music of her piano, and then silence provided the soundtrack to many, many more indiscriminate and beautifully moving moments framed on aging cranial celluloid. Visions of personal history, love, life, and a little magic had all inspired, perhaps with the echo of the universe. They'd conjured their own moment of hope frozen in the windmill of time just long enough for me to feel and to see.

Perhaps there was a reason for this. Perhaps these visions saved me from myself. They were momentary lapses of concentration during my acknowledgement of Carole's reality. She remained unable to respond to me. I was breaking and broken. The emergency services stayed on the phone with me until the ambulance arrived. Never have I felt so helpless, and in the moment, my heart surrendered to love never-ending.

A lone paramedic arrived first. The ambulance arrived a few seconds later. My daughter directed three medics upstairs as she'd been asked. They ascended two stairs at a time. She had done her job magnificently while comforting her younger brother.

I'd been awake now for about thirteen minutes or so according to the alarm clock on the bedside table. It was the longest thirteen minutes in the history of time and space and everything in between. I'd done all I could, but was it enough? My heart was telling me that it couldn't possibly be Carole's time – not like this, not now. Could it?

The team of medics swung calmly into action assessing Carole's condition. They talked loudly to her. Oxygen and tubes, machines and bags were opened, and a stretcher was left on the landing. I was worried for the children and left Carole momentarily. In the lounge, I let them know that everything would be OK. It had to be OK. I gave them a hug from both of us and then returned nervously to find no change. After a further fifteen minutes, Carole started to break her unconsciousness. She'd been transported to another dimension of reality for at least twenty-eight minutes, and no one could be sure how long before that.

As Carole woke, it was obvious that she was dazed and disoriented. The bedroom light was bright and shone in her eyes, causing her to blink repeatedly. Instinctively she put the back of her shaking hands to her face to block out the brightness. She then turned them over and wiped her brow symmetrically before hurriedly sliding both hands roughly up and down her grey cheeks as if to search for confirmation of her own physicality.

It was a few more seconds before the Carole I knew and loved began to re-emerge. She was surrounded by paramedics staring at her. They were talking softly, by this time with less anxious tone, asking questions, repeating her name, and looking for signs that she could hear and see them. Carole was semi-composed, or as composed as she could be. Her slender hourglass frame had become fragile and was clearly weakened by her temporary paralysis. Her body trembled as her hands and wrists sunk into the comfort of the mattress beneath as she tried to sit up in bed. She just about managed to support herself with both hands to find a comfortable seat. The female paramedic propped Carole up upon the re-plumped blood-stained pillows.

Initially, Carole couldn't speak from behind the foggy oxygen mask, which instinctively she tried to remove. Carole was mouthing very faint half-words as she fought to overcome breathlessness. The mask would, a few minutes later, be removed and replaced by two tiny nasal tubes. She glanced at her reflection in the mirrored wardrobe doors to her right and looked around the room and back at the mirror again. She did this several times, perhaps looking for signs of familiarity. She would have seen blood and saliva painted haphazardly along the right-hand side of her face. It stretched from the right corner of her lip along her jawbone to her earlobe and down her slender neck.

There was medical equipment on the bed and floor. She observed me wearing a T-shirt stained with her blood. She couldn't speak and had no idea why. She felt pain in her mouth, prompting her to explore it for a wound with the first two fingers of her right hand. She found her tongue and her own blood. She stared at her bloody fingers for a moment, holding her hand toward the light.

In the chaos of our room, Carole now looked frightened. She knew something was wrong but couldn't piece anything together. She was bewildered by all the close attention. I had to wait and spectate for a little while longer before I could go to her side. As time ticked on, my emotions fluttered between happy, sad, relieved, worried, and disbelieving. As I listened and observed, it became ever more painfully obvious that Carole's health was much cause for concern. My heart showed me Carole's vulnerability. It hurt.

Carole held out her arms as a child unconditionally requests a mother's love. I held Carole very gently in my arms. I can tell you that it was the most amazing feeling in the world. To this day, I treasure the memory. I stroked the back of her head deftly with my right hand and with the other embraced her bare back beneath a damp cotton nightshirt scented with the fragrance of illness and Carole's sweet perfume. I could hear blood rushing through the chambers of her heart. It sounded like the drain cycle of a washing machine muffled with the sort of noise a child makes finishing the last slurps of bubbly milkshake through a striped paper straw.

I felt an odd sensation through my left forearm, like the vibration of water gushing full force from a bath tap inside her rib cage. Fluids gurgled in her upper torso and throat. Much blood and saliva had been swallowed during her desperation. She rested her heavy head on my left shoulder and wiped her bloody mouth on my T-shirt.

Very shallowly, and in three short gasps, Carole whispered, 'What ... just ... happened to me?' She hugged me so intensely around my neck that her elbows joined each other at the back of my head. She was still shaking.

I whispered very softly, 'We don't know – you're sick. I love you.' She stared at me like a little rabbit lost in the beam of car headlights. The lights must have been reflected in her eyes, which were now alive radially with the sharpest colour and deepest emotion. Despite her trauma, Carole's eyes were ever more vibrant with her inner beauty and passion for life. The love emanating from beyond the windows of her soul moved me in a way that I cannot describe with mere words, but to feel it was simply overwhelming. 'You had me a little worried there for a while,' I said. 'You had us all worried. Everything will be OK.'

There was a moment of silence before she managed to ask, 'Who are … these people and … why are they here?' I realised, hugging her on the bed, that Carole couldn't remember anything about the last twenty-eight minutes of her life. 'The children, where are the children?' she said.

I told her not to worry about the children. 'They're fine – worried about you, but fine.'

'Go get them, I want to see them, quickly,' she said with improving audibility.

Carole's primary instincts were always for her children. The love beamed from behind Carole's eyes as she hugged the kids, and a gentle sense of relief and perspective returned to me. She knew them. Mummy hugged them for a few seconds, conjured a big smile, and reassured them gently, telling them 'I'm OK, I'm OK.' They went back downstairs to the sanctuary of the lounge. Carole slumped back into her pillows and held her head in both hands as she looked skyward for inspiration.

The medics were still attending to Carole. They let me know that she needed urgent hospital care. I had to prepare a small overnight bag. She was to leave very soon in the ambulance. Carole was still bewildered by everything. Imagine waking up and having no recollection or understanding of events that threaten the beauty and wonder that is life, your life. No wonder she was confused.

Calmly and with a few escaping tears, which Carole brushed so delicately from my cheeks with butterfly's touch, I had just enough time to tell her about her missing twenty-eight minutes. Her eyes showed me that she was focused and attentive to my every word, listening with concerned but dreamlike disbelief. The expressions on Carole's face changed during our short conversation as though she was with me one minute but not the next and then back again. A look of horror, a smile, and horror again passed over as she struggled with her situation. The physical and emotional states of shock lifted her gently and then dropped her abruptly like a rock into my watery abyss of tears. Carole was exhausted as she drifted in and out of her reality.

'I must be dreaming,' she said.

I just shook my head slowly as she wiped my face again. I whispered to her, 'Trust me, you're not dreaming.'

'Don't cry,' she said. 'I'm OK, really, I'm OK.'

The brain is a clever machine, and on this occasion it had not failed Carole. It prevented her from remembering anything about her twenty-eight-minute struggle for breath. It shut down various bodily mechanisms to protect them from damage. That morning, it shut down nearly everything. It did its job. It switched off Carole's short-term memory to hide from her the horror of my visual theatre. She didn't see, as I had, her instinctive grasp for breath, for everything she loved.

Carole was still in shock, wondering what all the fuss was about. She knew where she was; she confirmed to the paramedics her personal information, name, age, etc. She had some idea of what had happened but still struggled to process the seriousness of it. Carole's eyes let me feel again her vulnerability despite their beauty and sparkle.

I précised very quickly for a second time what I had seen as she asked again very innocently, 'What just happened to me?' At the time, I put these temporary departures from her normally sharp cognisance down to her being in shock.

Carole probably wasn't in any way secure enough to walk down the stairs unaided, but she insisted that she was. In her own idiosyncratic way, with polite voice and stern expression, Carole refused point-blank any assistance. Aided only by the wooden banister, she negotiated a wobbly decent. I went downstairs backwards facing her despite her funny but purposeful rebuke. I was still in my blood-stained T-shirt, which caught her attention more harshly than before as she pointed wordlessly at the haphazard reddish saliva swirls everywhere.

We all stood in the middle of the street, the children in their dressing gowns and slippers. The night air was crisp, cold, and alight with stars twinkling through layers of gently rolling grey and indigo clouds. A strangely familiar landscape above the treetops appeared to have been painted sensitively with watercolour upon an emotional canvass of diamonds and tear drops. It was peaceful and strangely calm. I felt an odd sense of familiarity in the icy air. Maybe it was anticipation or expectation. Whatever it was, I can't forget. It was like déjà vu. I'd been there before. We had all been there before.

'Why am I going to hospital? I feel fine. Why is there blood on your T-shirt?' she slurred, pointing at me again. Carole was aware of the change in her speech, probably caused by the painful movement of her tongue as it attempted eloquent pronunciation.

We all shouted 'Love you!' as we waved her off.

The ambulance drove slowly and silently out of the street under blue flashing lights. The medics had been concerned primarily for Carole and hadn't said much to me. It was suggested that I phone the hospital in a few hours for an update. The duty registrar in the accident and emergency department would be my point of contact.

It was approximately four thirty in the morning. The children and I closed the front door and retreated to the safety of our little universe, our home. Everything was just a little odd, and my head was spinning as those fuzzy sparks and dots reappeared in my peripheral vision. I held my kids in the hallway at the foot of the stairs, one in each arm, and let my emotions run free in silence for just a few seconds, unable to reverse my waterfall. The children were calm – exhausted but calm – and naturally worried about Mummy. We all sat in the lounge and turned on the TV. I fetched their duvets and grabbed some food and drink, and we talked for a while. It was difficult to know what to say. I was only really conscious of trying not to frighten them any more than their own visual theatres may have done already.

We sat on the sofa for about twenty minutes, me in the middle with a child on either side. Their faces snuggled into my chest. I hugged them tightly, for me and for Carole. I tried to answer as many questions as I could, as delicately as I could. I kissed them both on the forehead twice – one kiss from Mummy and one kiss from me – and reminded them that Mummy and I loved them more than anything in the world.

At one point, I disappeared upstairs, grabbed a clean T-shirt, and escaped to the sanctuary of the bathroom, where I broke down quietly. I found myself sitting on the hard wooden floor behind the door. I'd tucked my legs up to my chest, arms wrapped around legs, nose buried between knees. I sobbed an ocean. Both relief and fear gripped me in that instant, as did the uncomfortable realisation that I was alone. For the first time in my married life, I was very alone – and scared.

Carole, too, was alone. My playback of the unconscious woman who had fought so hard to stay with me was painful and surreal. The lovely lady I knew so well maybe didn't know herself in quite the same way anymore. In my heart, I knew that all was not well.

In my isolation, I found it progressively more difficult to compute rationally the last hour of my life. In those lonely minutes behind the bathroom door, I realised how fragile life really is. Silence, realisation, and I were mutual companions for a little while. We forced each other with gentle foreboding to be grounded and aware so that best-case and worst-case scenarios could be acknowledged. What else could I do? My family needed me, so there were no other choices; besides, what doesn't kill you makes you stronger. Sounds odd, but I needed all the strength I could get. My little ones were waiting for me in the lounge on the sofa. Carole needed me to look after them, and anyhow, I'd do anything for my three best friends, anything and everything to keep them all safe.

Semi-composed and piggy-eyed, I dragged myself off the floor. For just a few more moments, I allowed myself to feel and to be broken – snapped in half like a dry twig. Slumped against the cold cream-coloured bathroom wall, I found myself staring into nothingness, trying to figure out what just happened. I washed my face in cold water and stared in the mirror at the reflection of a man I didn't know. A stranger stared back at me. He had bloodshot eyes which were half-closed, a brow more wrinkled than usual, an unshaven face, and a streaming nose. He'd aged some that morning. The stranger in the mirror was someone I'd become well acquainted with over time. He was to be my conscience, my demon, my salvation, my new nemesis, and strangely, my friend. We cried together in the early hours that morning. As I streamed our tears, he wiped my face. We ventured more deeply into the innermost sanctum of my heart and found honesty, acceptance, and love. We found Carole. It hurt like nothing I'd ever experienced before.

I returned to the children to find them curled up sleeping, one on either sofa. They were both in the foetal position, with toes and fingers sticking out of dressing gowns and duvets. I stared at them both, dropped to my knees, and sobbed quietly at their reality. I switched the lights off and lay on the floor in the lounge, keeping watch over my little braves. I replayed the horror of that morning in my head over and over again, seeking to rationalise love and life.

Carole was my world. We were each other's world. In those lonely hours, I acknowledged that our life as a family would never quite be the same. Uncertainty over the next few days unsettled me. I couldn't think past that; I'd accepted the situation for what is was but not necessarily what it might be. Practically, I knew that whatever it was had to be managed regardless of outcomes. It had to be managed. I'd have to manage it, and somehow I would.

Carole and I had always lived with a simple and straightforward 'it is what it is' approach to life. We believed that everything happened for a reason. Even when those reasons were not necessarily understood or were cruel, there would be moments in time thereafter that perhaps joined up some dots and made some sense. Even if there weren't, in those dotty moments of awakening we worked hard to make the most of whatever destiny had planned.

Our life together was always positive, always interesting, always happy, and above all else, always filled with fun and love. We'd cultivated a world of sense with sensitivity for each other and for all of us. Carole was always the sense in my nonsense, even when I was naturally over-sensitive. We had found a natural affinity in our own vulnerabilities, which we shared openly to make them strengths instead of weakness. We understood each other in every way.

All my life, I'd been able to read people, pick up on their feelings and intuitively know when things were good, bad, or just plain lovely. I'd notice simple things in the use of people's words or phrases, their body language, a look or a trusted gut feeling. Mostly I felt that people gave away their intentions, honesty, and deepest desire with their eyes, for our eyes reflect the music of the heart. I'd always been aware of this but never understood it quite in the way I did now. Carole had the most gorgeous eyes. That morning they sang the most beautiful song to me.

As I watched over the children for the next few hours, my senses stayed on super-alert, heightened to the extreme by the absence of my lovely wife. Carole and I would often sit in complete awe and adoration of the most amazing sight from time to time, which in our world was our sleeping babies. There is only one thing perhaps more angelic than a happy and contented sleeping baby, and that is a happy and contented lady blossoming with child. Carole was at her most naturally radiant and glowing when she carried our children through pregnancy. She did this with so much love – without doubt, it was the most beautiful thing I'd ever seen. To see and sense the love Carole had for her unborn babies, how she nurtured and kept them safe, was the most special experience to behold.

During our earliest days of parenthood, we didn't have to say anything to each other as we marvelled at the wonder of the little lives in front of us – their little fingers, the infant creases in their skin, their little toes and button noses, and that so lovely baby smell. To Carole and I, these things personified softness, perfection, and reason. We'd just hold hands and hug most evenings as we watched our babies sleeping.

Even though the children were older now, I watched over them during the dawning hours of our different morning in the same way, with so much unconditional love from both of us. As I traced the outline of their faces to memory, I realised just a little what it must be like to be a mother. I felt what I can only describe as maternal love, a unique bond, an inseparable emotional connection to the two little gifts asleep on the sofas.

In the lounge, my thoughts were still heavy and somewhat isolated as they raced this way and that. I had visual playback of Carole fighting to cling to life. Her blood was on her and on me, on my hands and T-shirt. Ironically, my memory was intact as it forced me to relive, over and over again, Carole's moments of greatest horror. Even though Carole was absent, I felt her presence in my thoughts and in my heart as I cared, as best I could, for our children.

The children were like Mummy in so many different ways. I tried to put myself in their shoes, and my thoughts drifted to their vantage point on the landing. What had they seen? I could only imagine how they might feel. How would they feel in the morning when they awoke to remember what had happened? They too would have playback and perhaps a dawning realisation that Mummy was not at home.

For the first time ever, I think, I was truly afraid. An icy shiver ran up my spine. I was consoled by the fact that Carole was a fighter who never gave up, laughed in the face of adversity, and just got on with life. She would be OK. I had to believe that she would be OK. We had each other and we had love. In my heart, I hoped that none of us would ever again endure our shared experiences of that morning.

The noise of the TV was interrupted abruptly by the ringing of the phone. The cream Victorian carriage clock on the brick fireplace read twenty to six. I hadn't slept. It was the duty registrar. My heart skipped a beat and then a few more. It raced without warning while trying to escape the knotted mess it had spasmed into throughout the early hours. The voice on the other end of the phone began to ask some fundamental questions, which re-engaged the earlier alarm bells.

'Can you tell me why Carole is in hospital? Carole does not know why she is here,' he said. I filled in the blanks for him, explaining the trancelike state I'd found Carole in, the injury to her tongue, and what appeared to be an absence of short-term memory. I was advised that Carole was awake on arrival. This was encouraging. However, the duty registrar expressed some concern that she couldn't recall how she'd travelled to hospital and had no idea why she was even there, and this worried me. It confirmed, yet again, that Carole still had no memory and had not regained her lost twenty-eight minutes. Could these minutes be lost forever?

It was now very apparent that she'd lost a few more minutes too. I was informed that Carole would remain in hospital for the day and probably the evening. The medical team needed to do some tests to establish what had happened and find the missing pieces of Carole's jigsaw of ill-health. I thanked the duty registrar for his call and let him know I'd make my way to Carole very shortly.

To Get to Know

I t was 3 May, 1993, a bank holiday Monday steeped in glorious sunshine. I awoke to find myself alone with my thoughts and a list of domestic chores to catch up on. I'd fallen behind with my work assignments and didn't really fancy doing the housework. I decided to make the small trip to the office where I could sit in quiet contemplation and write up my reports without distraction.

I'd regularly take on too much work on the basis that too much was always better than not enough. My accidental work ethic had always been along the lines of 'Some people achieve more when they have more to achieve.' It was always one of those things that's easy to say but difficult to do, and from time to time it served as a great escape clause when I really did have too much to do.

The car park was almost empty when I arrived. This was no great surprise, as it was a public holiday in the UK, the sun was shining, and the sky was blue – three things that were rarely heard in the same sentence! I should've guessed, really, that there would be something very different about that day, but like most people, I'd not made the time to stop and appreciate the clues.

I signed in at the front desk and had a short conversation with the security guard, who quizzed me about my purpose for being in the office on a day of paid holiday. He implied that I must be mad, rebuking me rather humorously for the fact that I had a choice not to work whereas he had no choice but to work. I made the point that we always have choices. He laughed as I headed for the lift to the first floor.

The office was in darkness and silence, apart from the dull mechanical drone of the lift departing. The sound of a teaspoon in a cup echoed around the floor. It reminded me of the ringing of a hand bell. The ringing noise was drowned out by the departure of the lift, so it was difficult to figure out where it was coming from. I turned right and switched on the lights, which flickered into life as I rounded the corner to the expanse of empty and uninspiring open-plan office.

To my surprise, a familiar face greeted me as I snaked between the large grey filing cabinets on my way to the hot-desk area. Sitting in isolation with only her thoughts for company was the loveliest girl, who'd arrived just a few minutes earlier. Her first priority had been a noisy cup of coffee. She greeted me with a friendly smile, remarking, 'Thanks for turning on the lights, Adrian. You saved me a job.'

I'd known Carole professionally for about eighteen months. She was the charming and organised girl with the quintessentially English accent who I spoke to every Monday morning on the phone. I'd update Carole with my itinerary for the week, place stationery orders, chase up my expenses, and provide updates to her on my management reports. Chatting to Carole had always been a very enjoyable experience. Occasionally, when my work took me into the unwelcoming office for meetings, Carole would offer to make me coffee. She did this for the rest of the team, but I didn't like to take advantage too often. I learned very quickly not to ask for tea – not her forte!

I had never really taken the time to get to know Carole, although she was someone who had previously caught my attention. I used to think that she had a nice bottom! I'd always held Carole in high regard as my very elegant and organised colleague with a lily-white freckled complexion who couldn't make tea. She was a happy-go-lucky girl in many ways, always smiling and always chatty. She fitted into any social or professional scene with ease, often with an opinionated but quietly sophisticated girly charm.

We were each as surprised as the other to find a colleague in the office and had the 'What are you doing here on such a lovely day?' conversation. We realised very quickly that we were there for some of the same reasons. Our domestic landscapes had converged into the same picture. Carole walked with me to the kitchen area as I went to make myself a coffee. As we chatted, I sensed that she might need a friendly ear. With coffee under grasp, on our way back from the kitchen I sat casually on the edge of her desk and listened as Carole began to tell me about her life. I'd never really spoken to her about anything other than work before.

After a short while, any thoughts of catching up on my assignments seized their opportunity to escape as I related to and empathised with an ordinary but very lovely girl. As we sat and talked … well, Carole talked mostly and I listened (boy, could she talk), time just slipped away. Time has a habit of doing this when you have wonderful company.

We shared our stories and were quietly surprised by the extent of synergy we found in our lives. We established that we'd lived and worked in some of the same parts of the UK at the same time. Our paths had been criss-crossing, so it seemed, for a while, and it was almost as if we were at some point destined to meet. Talking to each other was sort of effortless, and I had this very weird sense of déjà vu. I knew that Carole and I had met before, but I just couldn't place things together. It was sort of odd – but lovely odd, if that makes sense.

Some seven hours later, without a single word being typed on any of the mundane reports that were overdue, we decided it was probably a good idea to go back to our respective homes. Carole lived not far away, and I resided about twenty-five miles from the office on the outskirts of a sleepy village. Carole wrote down her phone number and handed it to me on a sticky note. I was taken aback by this – not because she handed me her phone number but because it was just one digit different from another phone number I already knew. I mentioned this, and we had a 'how weird is that?' moment, realising that perhaps fate had stepped into our lives that morning.

Perhaps life is just a beautiful journey of coincidences, and our bumping into each other that day was one of those. Whatever had been woven for the two of us to meet was a mystery that we would solve together twenty years on in our friendship. Something told us both separately that we were supposed to be in the office that morning. We trusted our inner feelings enough to just go with them, and I'm glad that we did. Sometimes, it takes just a little courage to trust our deepest instincts even when all the pieces of our jigsaws aren't in play or understood.

I'd always trusted my instincts and had tried to view life, rightly or wrongly, as a lesson of many lessons. I've always worn my heart on my sleeve, which can sometimes make the lesson a little tough. Carole had inside information, so to speak, that let her trust her feelings perhaps a little more than she would have usually, although I had no knowledge of that at the time we met in the office that day. We'd both left the office feeling differently about each other and about life, as a little ray of sunshine appeared very unexpectedly to reveal a horizon light of heart and very beautiful.

I followed Carole down the motorway for two junctions in my grey Astra. As my exit approached, I flashed my car headlights and we waved. Our ways parted temporarily, and I played back in my mind what had happened as I negotiated three counties of countryside on my way back to my sleepy hollow. The sun was still high and the sky still brightest blue. I had to pinch myself. It had been a day of sunshine in more ways than one. It was a day that started a very beautiful chapter in my life. It was a day of magical connection that began a journey that would never end and a love that would never die.

On this journey, Carole and I would see each other almost every day for the next eighteen and a half years. We would only ever be parted on a handful of days when I had overnight business trips. Perhaps there really was something intoxicating in the air that day that blew us together very gently on a breeze of butterfly kisses. Whatever it was, it was so lovely. Sometimes you sense when it's right to be with someone. Sometimes it's a moment when the world, your world, is at peace maybe for the first time or for the first time in a long time. It's one of the most wonderful feelings when the only thing you can think of is, *this just feels right*. When this happens, and you trust yourself just a little, it usually is, like another piece of a jigsaw finding its own place quite naturally into the evolving picture of your life.

Just two weeks after we'd sat and talked over coffee, Carole and I decided that we should explore the opportunity to get to know each other a little better. For me personally, I wanted to understand the sensation in my stomach every time I whispered Carole's name, every time I heard her voice, and always when I thought of her. Somewhere in those early weeks, we shared a moment which would somehow chart a course into the beautiful and the beyond.

We'd spent a few precious hours together making plans and drinking lemonade. As I dropped Carole off at her home, she paused for a moment of thought while she played with the silver buckle on the thin shoulder strap of her brown leather handbag. Even though we were still getting to know each other, I found the moment of silence in the car a little unfamiliar, because Carole nearly always had something to say. She did this weird thing with her mouth and pinned her bottom lip in place right of centre with her two front teeth. I didn't know if this was a good or a bad thing, and my heart skipped a few beats before she broke the momentary silence. I remember thinking, *I could listen to this girl talk for hours and never become bored, but why isn't she saying anything?* I guessed that whatever she was thinking about was important to her, and I decided to smile and wait. She looked at me with bright hazel eyes which she knew were probably revealing a little more than she had perhaps intended.

With the most wonderful glistening gaze, she unpinned her bottom lip and simply said, 'I feel very comfortable with you, Adrian – and I want you to know I like that very much.'

She kissed me very gently for a few seconds like I'd never been kissed before while she stroked the side of my face with her left hand. Then, with the grace of a swan, Carole glided out of the car. We said nothing else in that moment. We didn't need to. I couldn't anyway even if I'd wanted to. I had no words. Cupid's arrow had been dispatched with unearthly precision to find the open embrace of its intended recipients. Carole had found the key that opened up my heart with her kiss. As she closed the car door, we waved and smiled.

I drove away slowly, still very much in the moment. I watched Carole in my rear-view mirror as she walked with a spring in her step down the road and right into her driveway. The magnitude of that sublime moment hit me again like a little earthquake as I relived the sensual and lingering tingle of her kiss and the lightest of touches to my face. If I had been a cartoon character, there'd have been baby birds and butterflies flying in circles around my head against a backdrop of stars and cherubs playing harps by moonlight.

As I drove on autopilot for a few seconds with my imaginary companions, I said out loud, 'I am going to spend the rest of my life with this girl.'

* * *

As we spent more and more time together, we levelled each other's expectations and were honest about how we really felt. We let each other know quite quickly that we could talk about anything and everything in complete safety, with openness and with respect for our opinions, hopes, and fears. We discovered that we shared the same core values about life and about people. Above all else, we shared a pursuit of just one thing in dominion over all else: happiness.

I learned that Carole was a talented pianist, had a passion for the performing arts and musical theatre, and loved to dance. However, she lacked belief in her own musical abilities and only ever played her piano privately. No matter how much encouragement was lovingly bestowed upon her, Carole quietly refused to play publicly, choosing to share her raw talent only with those closest to her.

She had an athletic form and the longest legs I'd ever seen. She had a natural level of fitness which she balanced with deftly precise hand-eye coordination that was no doubt honed through her piano mastery. That said, Carole was not a huge fan of playing sport, despite physical and sensory gifts that would have served her well in any arena had she chosen sport as a vocation or career. Carole was pretty handy with a badminton racket just as long as you could stop her laughing long enough to play the odd point here and there!

She loved films that had a feel-good factor – the ones that were thought-provoking and stirred the cauldron of sensitivity and emotion, that perhaps restored your faith in compassion, love, and human kindness, that warmed your heart and sometimes made you cry. Her two favourite films of all time were the classic children's story *Mary Poppins* and *Beaches*. Walt Disney's other classic, *Bambi*, ran a close third and always made her cry.

She loved anything and anyone who could make her laugh. Carole always laughed; she loved to laugh and achieved this effortlessly, infecting anyone in her company. When Carole laughed, it was difficult not to laugh with her – almost impossible not to. Carole used to say that 'laughter is life's therapy.' She laughed with such intensity sometimes that she had to be reminded to breathe. It's said that laughter synchronises the internal organs of the body to achieve vibrational harmony and balance. Perhaps this energy of laughter is the reason why it's so infectious. If laughter really is one of life's therapies, then I guess Carole was a master therapist. She was my master of laughter!

In many ways we were alike, and yet in others we were the complete opposite of each other. I love sport, both watching and playing, and enjoy most racket and ball sports. I love art in its material form – drawings, paintings, sculptures, and photographs – but have very little interest in music or the theatre. The nearest I ever got to the stage was appearing in a primary-school production of Shakespeare's *A Midsummer Night's Dream*. I loved the lines adapted for our junior school's production, especially for my character; my favourite one-liner was, 'Come hither Puck, fetch me the flower called love-in-idleness.' These few words always conjure imagery of mischief and magic in an enchanted forest under the mystery of a silver moon and midnight's stars. Perhaps no relationship is ever complete without the characters of mischief and magic popping up every now and again to keep things interesting. On that day in the office, I think Puck had perhaps found the flower that reawakened idleness and made of opportunity his master's mischief.

When we first met, Carole had a few hard edges that I quietly and invisibly softened. Sometimes she was a tough cookie, and occasionally just a little tougher than she needed to be. Carole, in turn, galvanised my marshmallowy exterior into something a little more protective and useful. We did this without loss of our collective sensitivities. I used to call her 'my little armadillo' because once it was possible to see through Carole's self-styled carbon-fibre exterior, it was plain to see that she was squishy and cuddly on the inside. Naturally, if you ever saw through Carole's armour plating, it was because you were granted, by her, this privilege. When I thought maybe Carole worked her armoury in the negative, I would simply say 'armadillo', and she'd understand exactly what I was messaging to her.

At her core, Carole was determined and unflappable, and she possessed a well-meaning desire for fairness to herself and to others. Her sense of fair play and integrity radiated with the same clockwork precision that the sun rises and sets every day. She employed this in her professional and social lives and struggled sometimes with those who weren't tuned into her same station of philosophy or value.

Like most of us, Carole would tell you that she learned some really hard lessons along the way that gave her the treasure of appreciation for the special people at the core of her life. She intuitively knew when things were out of balance and assumed a mediatory role to restore equilibrium to many a situation of inner and outer conflict. She'd happily chat through the merits of each scenario and the characters involved, and paint a lyrical landscape of the bigger picture. Usually, if not always, Carole was in the right area. She had a knack for offering persuasive context to end up morally ascendant without realising it, and I think this was perhaps one of her lovely vulnerabilities as well as a great strength. Sometimes this rendered the other point of view weak or just irrelevant because it had been disproved and thus no longer had basis or substance in fact or contextual debate.

This gentle idiosyncrasy often revealed itself when she played chess. Carole's white queen commanded strategic and intellectual alliance of all her pieces many moves ahead of her playing partner until checkmate was in sight and her natural instinct for fair play overcame her desire to win. This was often a source of personal frustration for Carole and a very beautiful metaphor for her own compassionate nature.

I loved her diplomacy and sometimes her lack of it – her directness and her openness which, wherever possible, she complemented with a natural sensitivity towards others that balanced the unbalanced and rationalised the irrational. She didn't always get things right, but she did have an internal barometer that wouldn't let her rest until a degree of harmony had been achieved for all concerned. She would stress behind the scenes about the life stuff that she wanted to change but found it difficult sometimes to influence things to her satisfaction. Once she realised that the fundamental principles of managing stress on a daily basis lay in the sanctuary of her own mind, she was much more accepting of that which she couldn't change and ever more determined about that which she could.

Carole was a true Libra who worked hard to keep her life balanced, with boundless positive energy that hardly ever waned.

To most of us, she was just plain old Carole: opinionated, charming, girly-rude but so funny with it. She never took herself or life too seriously. She was in love with life and cultivated a life of love for everyone she cared about. One of her favourite personal expressions was 'Just be yourself – life's too short to be anyone else.'

She was the person who didn't care what you looked like or where you came from or who your friends were. She had no regard for any of the things that divide the world of friendship and love into distasteful and unnecessary oxymoron. She didn't care about your life choices and certainly not about your relationship preferences – only your friendship. Carole would say that *love knows not gender, love only knows love.* Carole had an internal antenna that was a sort of X-ray machine where friendship and love were the only source of reflective and inflective energy.

As we invested time in each other and for each other, we began to lay the foundations upon which we could build a relationship that would give us both what we wanted. We both dreamed of happiness. We worked hard to figure this stuff out but made it an activity drenched in sunshine and lots of fun. Perhaps we also learned lessons from our own personal histories to work through those early days carefully, understanding, appreciating, and sharing with each other the really important things so that we could shape our future in the way we wanted. Maybe it was a little bit of many things and some courage and trust thrown in for good measure.

There were many moments during the first two or three weeks when it would have been very easy to walk away from each other. We made things unnecessarily bumpy in lots of ways, but as we surfed each wave of challenge, we found it easier to walk along our metaphorical beach and enjoy the magic of every sunset together. Sometimes clearing a path to be able to see where you're going is a difficult, emotional, but worthwhile thing to do. As we started clearing, planting, and building together, we realised something very natural and wonderful was taking root in the dandelion garden of life. I'd found someone with rare qualities and a love of life, a mostly gentle self-assuredness, and gorgeous smiling eyes. Carole would always carry the weight of her world on her shoulders, and throughout my association with her, she rarely deflected her fears outward or used them destructively on others. As we grew together, Carole slowly let me share the weight, and between us we would learn to lighten the other's load when needed.

I will always remember the very first time Carole whispered those magical words 'I love you' in my ear. We were standing in the kitchen in total darkness when a little light flickered between us as if to illuminate the way. I had my hands around her slender waist and was about to kiss her when she threw her arms around me as tight as you like and softly let those magical words escape her heart. Needless to say, I whispered four magical words back through her long auburn hair as we shared an almost mystical gaze. I still get goose bumps, even now, when I close my eyes and relive that beautiful moment – the moment our souls began to talk to each other. My life has never quite been the same since, and I now know it never will be again.

On summer evenings in 1993, we'd take off in the car with a picnic and no other plans. Carole and I would make tuna, mayo, and onion sandwiches. We'd remove the crusts, cut the sandwiches into triangles, and wrap them in greaseproof paper. Fruit juice or fizzy water, chocolate, and crisps completed our feast for two. Picnic blanket in the trunk, we just pointed the car and off we went into the sunshine.

We ended up in all sorts of places. One of our favourite destinations to relax became Henley-on-Thames in Oxfordshire. We'd either picnic by the river or walk along it, eating ice-cream and holding hands as we watched the river traffic negotiate safe passage. Sometimes we'd pop into the Angel on the Bridge for a drink and occasionally a bite to eat. We talked about all sorts of things, painting each other's canvas with images of past, present, and future.

Often on our way back home on those warm summer evenings, we'd find a quiet spot in the middle of nowhere, park the car, and do something that most people would probably find slightly unusual. We'd lie on the car bonnet with our backs against the windscreen, cuddle up together, and just gaze into the myriad of stars twinkling in the midnight sky. We'd try to figure out the mysteries of what might lie behind the cosmos in faraway places.

Carole would point out one or two of the more well-known star groupings. Her personal favourite was an asterism of seven stars found in the Ursa Major constellation called the Plough, or sometimes Charles's Wain in the UK. I thought this poetic, as Carole's maiden name was also 'Wain' – another one of those mysterious coincidences perhaps. The Plough is known in many parts of the world as the Big Dipper, the Seven Goddesses, or the Bureaucrat. It is one of the brightest and most easily identifiable patterns in the sky. To me, it always looked like a giant supermarket trolley.

I don't know why, but from early childhood, the moon and the night sky had always been a mystical thing of wonder in my life. It was lovely to find out that the universe starred as brightly in Carole's fascination as it did my own. Today, I can't wander outdoors at night without centring my energies with the moon and locating my shopping trolley in the sky.

A little like the universe, Carole and I were finding that our energies worked well most, if not all, of the time. When she pushed, I pulled; when in opposition, we mostly attracted, and with any rare occasion of forces repelling, we granted each other all the time and space in the world to work things out considerately and so avoided potential argument and misunderstanding with ease. Sure, we disagreed on loads of stuff, but we did this with respect for each other's position through our awareness of love and happiness in ascendency over being proved right or wrong.

I guess this was a sort of a no-blame culture that sat comfortably with us where there were no losers or winners, just a little slice of wisdom that, over time, meant that everyone prevailed undamaged, happy or happier. Mostly we were perfectly aligned in our own interplanetary configuration and taught each other the benefits of being acutely aware of all of the dynamic forces and energies that challenged and harmonised us every day. We built upon these foundations subconsciously and learned from each other and our experiences, seeing most things as opportunities instead of threats or disappointments.

* * *

One Sunday in June 1993, we'd been invited out to lunch. Carole's aunt and uncle on her mother's side of the family lived about an hour's drive away on the south coast of England. We took a leisurely drive in the mid-morning heat, enjoying the landscape of a scenic route we'd chosen quite randomly on our way over. Carole had taken this journey many times as a child when the two families would get together every few weeks to catch up with each other and with life. They'd always enjoy their time together over a traditional three-course roast dinner – preceded, of course, by an aperitif or two of a favourite tipple.

This was the first time I'd had an opportunity to formally meet any of Carole's extended family, so a few nerves travelled with us that morning. Carole's aunt was called Bernadette, and Carole referred to her always as Tata. We arrived shortly after midday, making good time despite the spontaneity of our route planning. The country lanes had been relatively quiet and our journey incident-free, so we were both fairly relaxed. After some lovely home-cooked French cuisine, we all decided to take a walk through the Hampshire countryside and explore a little more the intentions of nature.

Not far from Tata's house, Carole and I found ourselves walking hand in hand through a meadow of tall grasses and fragrant wild flowers. The pollen-scented air was animated abundantly with the flutter of cabbage-white butterflies and the sound of busy bees. I've always loved butterflies – something about their time-dependent transformation as a perfection of nature. A warm and gentle breeze accompanied us to cool the effects of the afternoon sun.

As we walked, we talked with Tata about this and that and how Carole and I had met. She wanted all the details. It took me a little while to realise that Tata was actually on a secret mission to assess my potential suitability. I wasn't sure if this was a carefully constructed plan involving one other would-be matchmaker or if Tata was flying solo. Either way, she was planting seeds and dropping hints. I think it was eventually the regularity, forthrightness, and intensity of her twenty-plus questions that gave away her game of mischief. My every word had endured scrutiny of the deserving kind.

Once I figured out what was going on, I let Tata know how I felt about Carole, and then she let me know that she already knew. She said, 'I can see it in your eyes, and in Carole's too.'

Tata would later tell me that she had simply been exploring the possibility that we hadn't yet seen this for ourselves. What I hadn't seen was that a plan was in full flower to achieve a particular objective, of which Tata's own matchmaking mischief was the first of two carefully thought-out phases. Clearly, Tata had inside knowledge too!

It was during our meadow conversations that I learned Carole had been adopted shortly after her birth. Carole hadn't mentioned this to me, and I guess that if she'd wanted to or had purpose to, then she would've done. I'm not sure why, but these curiously insignificant details made me love her even more. Carole was always a private person, and she was shrewd enough to drip-feed information to new people in her life as she first established their friendship and their trustworthiness.

When we arrived back at the house, my new best friend for the day stole me away from Carole for a few minutes. Carole sat in the garden on a wooden bench, alone with her thoughts. The sun was still shining and the sky was still blue. Behind Bernadette's glasses, I noticed a glint of mischief again – the sort of excited look found in children's eyes when they are about to do something that they know they probably shouldn't but they just can't stop themselves. I was not disappointed, as she ushered me out of Carole's view and promptly handed me something. The smile in her eyes was by this time accompanied by a very cheeky grin. Tata had plucked a flower from her garden. It was a single rose of deepest crimson and beautiful of form.

With a wink, a nod, and a hand gesture in Carole's direction, she simply said, 'Off you go!'

I stared at my rose for a few seconds and then glanced at the flower in my hand. Both were perfectly formed and just beginning to reveal their inner beauty. Tata concealed herself behind the kitchen window to observe at a distance the defining moment of my life. I was calm on the outside and nervously excited at the opportunity handed to me in the moment. My inner child was jumping. Without a second thought, sensing that what I was about to do *just felt right*, I walked toward the garden bench to my very own love-in-idleness, the rose concealed behind my back.

I found my lovely girl smiling in quiet contemplation. The sun had kissed her lily-white complexion through the afternoon breeze, exploding a glow of freckles about her face. She was a vision of loveliness as time stopped just for a moment, long enough for me to see, to feel and to know. Her chameleon hair of burnt auburn with rich dark brown and naturally tinted orange tones was roughly tied back in a ponytail by a brown velvet scrunchy. Strands of loose curly hair feathered gently in the breeze across her face, catching between her lips. She removed her brown-rimmed tinted sunglasses from their perch of perfect symmetry across the bridge of her freckly nose. Her sunglasses found gentle rest on the top of her head, acting as a temporary hairband to keep the ticklish stray hair off her face.

With one hand behind my back and without a single word, I dropped to one knee and lost myself for a moment in Carole's sparkly hazel eyes. She laughed and then, laughing again nervously, she said 'What are y—?' She realised mid-sentence as I held her hand and, with my other hand, presented the rose.

I whispered, 'Carole, you know I love you – I want to spend the rest of my life with you. Will you …?'

Before I could complete the question, Carole said, 'Yes!'

Her reply was accompanied by even more nervous laughter. Her hand was shaking just as much as mine as she accepted the bloom. She consumed its fragrance and kissed it, pausing for a moment, looking at me and back to the object of my affection in her left hand. And then she kissed me. In my cartoon world, we were serenaded by my imaginary companions on delicate wings animating love on her breeze of enchanted symphony, of harps, and violins. The memory of Carole's kiss and my vision of her loveliness will stay with me beyond the mirrors of time. It journeys always in my heart through the doors of my own perception in a place where there is no matter and all that matters is love. I'd found my soulmate, my English rose.

From her seat on the bench, she looked for her aunty, who was no longer hiding in the kitchen.

'Did you know about this?' she exclaimed as Tata advanced the few steps toward us with outstretched arms. 'I knew you two were up to something, I just knew it – all those questions!'

Kisses and hugs of the loveliest kind were exchanged in the sunshine. There was more nervous laughter. And then there was even more nervous laughter.

Driving home that afternoon, there was only one thing on our minds. We talked a lot about the events of our special day; even though they'd taken us a little by surprise, we concluded that spending the rest of our lives together was something that just felt very natural and very right. I couldn't explain it, other than to say that after spending those seven short hours with Carole in the office on bank holiday Monday, there was, in my mind, a sure-fire inevitability about spending the rest of my life with her.

I'd never really examined the philosophy of falling in love or even love at first sight before and never imagined in my wildest dreams that I could feel as happy or as loved as I did on that afternoon and for the rest of my life. Carole felt the same, although she had intuitive insight on matters of the heart. This was something that would slip her memory for at least the next ten years, maybe longer. Carole was a little forgetful sometimes, but it was just one of the beautiful perfections that made her who she was.

Carole's Mum got the news of the day via the hot-wire that was Tata's phone while we journeyed home, and she was in a relaxed state of mild excitement by the time we arrived back. I think she may have been the silent partner to Madame Mischief. On the day following my rose presentation, I asked Carole's father for his daughter's hand in marriage. Oddly, I hadn't finished asking the question before he too replied in the positive. We toasted the occasion with a glass of very fine Scotch before the girls joined us – another lovely moment.

Over the next few weeks, there was an excitement about life that we'd never experienced before. There was a future. Sounds odd, doesn't it? My life, our life, had a future. I suppose our lives had always had a future, just with a few missing pieces to find and slot into place. Life had taken on new meaning, new purpose, and a new perspective, and it was lovely. In the middle of what I realise now, while writing, was a very ordinary chapter, a fairy tale fluttered quite innocently to us on a gentle rose-scented breeze that June day. I had found one of the pieces that fitted my jigsaw. In Carole, I had found a soft, caring, and spirited girl who I knew I wanted to spend the rest of my life with. And Carole had found herself. Maybe she'd found her inner butterfly. I simply adored her.

During our lives together, we would discover many more of our own pieces of two very separate jigsaws. We'd find pieces of different shape, size, dimension, depth, and complexity. We soon worked out that our two jigsaws were no longer separate pictures but one giant landscape of adventure with hills to climb, fields to plough, winding roads to travel, and valleys and waterfalls against a backdrop of blushing sunsets, silvery moons, and a million stars. It was a landscape we could creatively fuse by being together. Pieces we couldn't find weren't necessarily missing; perhaps they were just dormant, waiting patiently in the wings of our theatre of dreams to make their entrance at the right moment and for the right reason. Happiness, understanding, and love had started to spread themselves evenly through many more layers of our fabric. Life wouldn't always be a picnic because, well, it's not supposed to be – and besides, where's the fun in that?

A few weeks later, sometime in July, after a busy week at work, we decided to spend Friday evening at the cinema. We arrived early and hadn't looked at what was showing in advance. I can't actually remember which film we bought tickets for. We had about forty minutes to fill before the film started, so we popped next door to the bowling alley and grabbed seats at an empty table in the busy bar. While we decided what to drink, Carole seemed somewhat preoccupied.

'What's on your mind? What's up?' I asked.

'Oh – just thinking, girly stuff! Nothing really ... well, just my dress.'

'Hold that thought,' I said. 'Tell you what, you draw your dress on the back of that napkin.' I pointed to a paper napkin folded in half on the table in front of Carole 'and I bet I can describe what you've drawn when I get back from the bar.'

'Bet you can't,' she replied.

I just looked at her and went, 'Try me!'

I grabbed a beer and Carole's usual non-alcoholic drink without ice and arrived back at our table about ten minutes later. Carole had drawn her ideal wedding dress on the napkin, which was now folded in half again and concealed between the palm of her right hand and the table.

Carole looked at me as I sat down, and I could tell what she was thinking: something like *he's gonna get this so wrong!*

'You ready to find out if I know you as well as I think I know you?' I asked, smiling at her.

'Yeah, right,' she mocked, but in a nice way.

I closed my eyes for a few seconds and focused on my breathing. Through a simple thought process, I drew in a single breath and felt its journey through to the back of my nostrils and into my head, where it diverged above and below. I imagined the downstream sensation of air inflating my chest and swirling vapour-like into my heart, causing a tingly sensation. It was like being kissed sensually on the back of my neck. It sent goose bumps pulsating deliciously in spontaneous rhythm up and down my spine. The upstream flow caused a dreamy light-headedness to fuse the sensations of heart in mind in body.

I imagined Carole in her wedding dress. I let my heart do my thinking for me, and then I saw her. I saw a princess with her hair coiled and curled mostly off her face with ringlets that escaped and suspended spring-like shoulder-length on either side. I saw her dress. With this image fixed firmly, I opened my eyes and was very quickly back in the noisy bar, still a little light of head.

Carole was laughing. 'You make me laugh,' she said. 'You're bonkers!'

I probably was bonkers, but I guessed that even if I got this wrong, it would be something we'd talk about for years to come. I'd have to be the butt of a few jokes and a few laughs, but no harm done – a bruised ego, perhaps, but nothing more. She'd love me anyway because I'd make her laugh, so nothing to lose really and everything to gain. If I got it there or thereabouts, I guess my ego lived to fight another day.

'Right then, here goes.' I began to describe the fairy-tale image fixed firmly behind my eyes. 'I see your hair is curly and you're wearing it up – probably irrelevant but wanted to mention. The dress is white and sleeves are three-quarter length; they're long but not all the way down to your wrist. The upper part of the dress and the sleeve is lace of the softest pattern, nothing too over the top. The lace also covers the upper part of the dress over a bodice that is probably boned at the back; I can't see the back but that's what I feel. Oh – and there are three V shapes, and the skirt is elegantly shaped but it's not a meringue, maybe white or ivory, probably white. How did I do?'

Carole was laughing again, only this time it was nervous laughter – and lots of it, just like the laughter in Tata's garden. It took her a few seconds to turn the napkin over, but as she did, she kept her hand over something she'd written. We both stared at her drawing, which actually was quite detailed. The skirt was princess-like in shape but not overstated. There was lace, long sleeves, and a bodice tapered to the waist in a V at the front.

I can't write down exactly what she said, for obvious reasons, but it was along the lines of, 'How the … did you do that?' She added, 'I didn't draw the back, but I would want it boned like a Basque!'

She moved her hand to reveal the two words she'd written down underneath her picture. They read, 'Hair up.' She reached out her arms and hugged me. 'I love you' was whispered in my ear, and then she said, 'Let's go home. Now I know I'm supposed to marry you!' I sat there for a moment thinking I'd struck gold when Carole broke my daydream with a girly smile and a sparkle in her eyes. 'Let's just go and plan our wedding right now!' What could I say? Not exactly what I was imagining 'let's go home' to mean in my overactive and very imaginative one-track mind!

What I did say, because this is the sort of thing a guy would say, was, 'What about the cinema tickets?'

'I've got an idea,' she said. 'Let's find a couple in here who look like they're in love and give them the tickets!'

I'm thinking, *You mean sell them the tickets!*

'Come on, let's go!' she said.

As we left our drinks, she grabbed my hand and off we went in search of a couple who looked like they were supposed to be together. Sitting at the bar just a short distance away were a guy and a girl who looked perfect together. Carole matter-of-factly marched over to them, apologised for the interruption, and offered them the tickets, explaining briefly that we were spontaneously in wedding-planning mode. While this wasn't the sort of thing you do every day, it was one of those 'must do now' things, and it felt right. Besides, who knows, maybe we passed on some good fortune that evening. I hope we did.

Carole said to them, 'I hope these tickets bring you much luck.'

I think we caught the couple off guard, and they seemed a little uneasy, maybe awkward, about accepting the tickets, but they thanked us and wished us good luck. We left them at the bar chatting about the free tickets. In our own excitement, we'd misplaced the napkin but not the dress design, which was by this time tattooed in two memories for safekeeping.

On our way home, we stopped off at the local store and bought cookies of the double-chocolate-chip variety – Carole's favourite. For the rest of the evening, we shared a lovely understanding over several cups of coffee and a few packets of cookies. Carole never quite looked at me in the same way again – I think this was a good thing. She'd ask me many times over the course of our succeeding years together how I did what she called 'the wedding-dress thing'.

I'd always give her the same answer: 'One day I'll tell you!'

For the remainder of the weekend, our bedroom floor was a sea of bridal magazines, handwritten notes, and sticky notes that changed places many times on seating plans. Lists began to form of all the things we needed to think about and do. We also made a decision on the date for the wedding after lots, and I mean *lots*, of deliberation. I wanted Carole to pick the date. I wanted her to have the freedom to choose which of the four seasons she felt the most affinity with. Winter or spring were Carole's first choices, because her heart's desire from childhood was to be a snow queen married against a picture-postcard backdrop of falling snow in a magical winter wonderland. We provisionally pencilled in the third and fourth weeks of January 1995. Autumn was the next choice, as this was Carole's favourite time of year. We weren't totally convinced that the weather conditions would be kind … like they'd be any kinder in January? Summer was discounted more or less straight away, as Carole disliked the heat even though she loved sunshine.

Finally, after we'd reviewed the logistics and chatted about all the practicalities, Carole opted for a date in the early autumn of 1994. She chose September, the same as her birth month. Carole's wedding dress, of course, had already been decided, along with her hair! We both felt like fate had again stepped into our ordinary world to guide us through the next year or so of our life. The coincidental synergy of our thoughts about her wedding dress was one of those lovely things that bonded us ever more tightly in love's embrace.

Carole would refer to that moment in the bar at the bowling alley for a very long time thereafter. It had intrigued her so much, capturing a notion of romance with a little splash of mystery. To her it was a sign, perhaps, of something that related to information about her life that she'd received from a stranger before we'd met. Maybe it was just that, or maybe it was something else. I like to think that Lady Synchronicity was looking out for us both that day with a guiding hand that held the keys to a lifetime of enchanted dreams.

We finally made it to sleep in the early hours of Saturday morning after many cups of coffee and an obscene amount of cookies. We had just over a year to get everything together, and many more late nights followed as we planned, organised, and replanned our big day.

Anyone who has been married or is planning to get married knows that it is billed as one of the most memorable days, if not *the* most memorable day, of your life. Once you announce your wedding intentions, everyone and his dog is just so pleased for you. Everywhere you go, people want to offer you all the advice under the sun for achieving the perfect day and a lifetime of happiness. They volunteer this information to you out of love and kindness, sometimes when you don't want to hear it because you've heard it a million times before. In all cases, though, its advice offered with nothing other than good intentions and love – after all, isn't that what marriage and life is all about? The single most important piece of advice I received was a simple but defining one: enjoy the day and absorb each other in it boundlessly because it will be over in a flash.

Carole insisted that she and her Mum would go dress hunting, so I happily left them to it, although I was slightly disappointed that tradition ruled against us undertaking this particular pleasure together. I wanted Carole to get the wedding dress that she really wanted and figured that a change in mind might take her design preferences into another direction altogether. Of course, it was her prerogative to change her mind. Even though I kind of already knew what her ideal dress would look like, Carole played a humorous guessing game with me all the way up to our wedding day. She wanted to retain an element of surprise and wonder for the first moment I saw her bridal loveliness. In an ideal world, Carole would walk down the aisle in the dress scribed on the napkin and inspired by simultaneous thought process and the interconnectedness of heart, mind and body. In my world of ideals, I knew that whatever Carole chose to wear, she would be perfect.

There was, of course, one other very special task I had to look after. I'd decided not to canvass Carole for her ideas or preferences. Given my success with 'the wedding-dress thing', I figured I'd be more or less safe to make this other design decision on my own. I wanted to purchase this particular item with a degree of thoughtful creativity in a way that my choices would mirror some of the characteristics of its new owner.

My creative inspiration would eventually arrive from two sources: the midsummer sky and music. I wanted something that twinkled like the stars but was also as understated and as beautiful as the moon's halo. Something that would never date but would remind Carole of the defining moment she changed my life forever. I also wanted to incorporate carrots into the theme in a quirky but very subtle acknowledgement of the nickname she'd lovingly bestowed upon me. I trawled the shops and then trawled them some more until I found what I was looking for in a shop window on Northbrook Street. The gift arrived just a few weeks later after being resized, and I made a very special trip to collect it.

That same evening, I proposed again to Carole on one knee in a very private moment, using the lines from an infamous poem that starts 'roses are red, violets are blue.' It ended with, 'I'd love to spend the rest of my life with you.' Carole loved the simple beauty of her very plain solitaire diamond set in eighteen carat gold, telling me that it was exactly what she'd have chosen. I loved it because the real jewel was not set in the ring but embedded in the heart of the lady who wore it and laid bare on the seamless sleeve of the gentleman who adored it.

In honour of our very special moment that evening, we would use the 'roses are red, violets are blue' theme for writing silly but heartfelt poems on the inside of cards to each other that marked special occasions, including St Valentine's day, birthdays and anniversaries. If we were feeling particularly creative, several verses would be written in silly language on the envelopes. Despite the humour of our poetry from time to time, there was a serious vein of thought running through the few lines of sentimental whisper I'd used to propose with the ring. Red roses are said to be the favourite flower of the Goddess of Love, Venus – appropriate, given our fascination with the mysticism of the night sky. I'd initially proposed in Tata's garden with a crimson rose, and roses are associated with St Valentine. Everything converged back to the personification and metaphor of love, hence my English rose, the object of my desire, my love, and my love for Carole.

And, just for anyone with a wildly creative imagination for romance, passion, and a little mischievousness, there exists a beautiful floral connection between Shakespeare's very own mischief-maker Puck and Eros, the Greek God of Love. Perhaps Puck and Eros are one and the same, balancing love in all its guises, jesting comedic notations and serious emotional hyperbole through the rose-coloured glasses of mystical intoxication. Love-in-idleness is another name for a particular variety of pansy that derives root from the French word *pensées*, which translated into English means 'thoughts'. Love-in-idleness translates into love in thought – dreams of the heart, midsummer nights of dreams. Curiously, and perhaps perfectly poetic, is that the name given to the mischievous Greek God of Love for his name is an anagram of 'rose', the flower of love. Carole was the seed of my dreams, my flower of love.

* * *

The next year literally flew by. As well as absorbing ourselves in all things matrimonial, we also bought our first house and would move into it when we arrived back from honeymoon. It had been a year of change, a very happy year in which we hadn't really stopped to think about what we were doing. We'd found ourselves in the flow of love's embrace. We'd found each other. It felt as if we were two long-lost friends blossoming on the canvas of our own wild-flower meadow of heartfelt wishes and enchanted kisses. Without realising it, we had accidentally created a theme that touched many elements of our wedding day in a way that would reflect the canvas we were painting together.

Our three-tiered wedding cake had roses of pink decorative icing. The same elegant design was featured on the fabric of the three bridesmaids' dresses. Carole's bouquet was made fresh of them and the table decorations were made of them, as were the buttonholes. All were coordinated of subtle candyfloss pink and white pastel. That is, apart from the twelve red ones I sent to Carole wrapped in a ribbon and bow during her morning of hair-up and make-up. And, of course, I was marrying the loveliest and fairest rose of them all.

Our big day – Saturday, 3 September, 1994 – arrived very quickly, and there were roses everywhere! We'd managed to balance, I think, the excitement of marriage with the sense of occasion. We wanted our guests to enjoy the day with us just as much as we knew we would enjoy the day with them. Carole had been the driving force for getting things organised, and she was the one who made everything happen. She made lots of the decisions, working very closely with her Mum on all matters, and between them they'd done an amazing job. Everything fell into place – that is, apart from the weather. It was a day of rain, but no one seemed to notice the puddles of rainbow chalk refracting on the pavement or the clouds of silver linings in the sky.

According to time-honoured tradition, I didn't see Carole or her wedding dress before the ceremony proper, nor did I see Carole for very long the evening before, as we spent a strange day and night apart. It was strange because it felt wrong not to be together, albeit for the right reasons. My best man and I put finishing touches on speeches at three in the morning in the hotel lobby while the night concierge ensured our beer glasses were never empty. It's actually quite scary just how much a speech can change in the time it takes to drink a beer or three.

I didn't sleep much during the early hours and only just managed to keep my nerves in check. Just after midday, time was upon us to walk the short way from the hotel to the church. We arrived in good time for a photo opportunity at the Lychgate with our two professional photographers and a pair of matching wedding rings. Our professionals for the afternoon were family friends whom Carole had known for several years. They were the father and sister of one of Carole's loveliest and closest friends, Mandy, who, with her husband Paul, were also our guests that afternoon.

Mandy had very kindly offered Carole and I a choice of wedding present. Carole had, unselfishly, chosen a very fluffy blue-point Birman kitten over a professional portfolio of wedding photographs. Whispa, our kitten, was the first of many wonderful special-day gifts. As our remaining guests started to arrive with brollies and coats, so time quickened upon us to take our seats.

Whispered sentiments of excitement and anticipation announced the arrival of the girl, of my English rose. A collective love of thoughts and imaginative companions played serenade in a stir of silent echoes reverberating through the lofty rafters. There was a moment of universal symphony, with swishing hats and turning heads fused in time with the movement of shuffling feet and creaking pew. I closed my eyes and dared to dream. With deepest breath, so started music that cast enchanted kisses of love's own wishes through veiled loveliness.

Carole tiptoed gracefully into view behind me. I didn't turn around as she neared me. I didn't have to. The downstream sensation of swirling vapour-like butterflies condensed in concert with the sensual tap of mischief's wand on the back of my neck. Spine-tingling magic confirmed the arrival of that which my heart already knew. At my side there stood the loveliest girl, an elemental princess. Her beautiful form was animating a dress of napkin-designed perfection, illustrated by the '*pen*' that '*sees*' only the flower of love. I mouthed the words 'I love you,' and she smiled with her eyes in a moment forever etched in the locket of two hearts.

3

To Love and Grow

At seven o'clock, I rang Carole's parents and explained our situation. I relived for the umpteenth time the events of our anxious early morning. Meanwhile, the children had been awake for about thirty minutes and were, as far as I could tell, coping. They were in the lounge snuggled in their duvets together eating a breakfast of chocolate, yoghurt, sliced apple, and cranberry juice – a family favourite. On the phone, we agreed that I could drop the children off post-haste. The three of us got ready in double-quick time. Time was becoming an ever more important part of life.

I'd packed Carole's mobile phone in her small bag of personal items and made sure it was switched on. I rang Carole just before we left home to let her know that I was on my way. In typical Carole fashion, she asked again what she was doing in hospital only this time there was humour in her voice.

'Bun, why am I in hospital? There is nothing wrong with me!' I could tell that she was feeling a little better, as she asked me to bring some sweets and chocolate and something decent to eat. 'I'm starving!' she said. 'I'm staring at a bowl of breakfast cereal soaked in warm milk! Yuck!'

The other thing she did was ask about the children. It was the loveliest feeling in the world to hear Carole's voice in familiar tone. Her questions were my calming sunshine. A storm had thundered into our lives from literally nowhere that morning. It threatened my family with clouds of crimson tears across a dark rolling indigo sky. It was still raining in my heart. I could cope with just a little rain.

Standing in the kitchen of Carole's childhood home, I urged her Mum not to worry. One of those things, I guess, which is easy to say but impossible to do. Mums worry constantly, no matter how old their children are. I committed to giving regular updates throughout the day as we each set sail upon a sea of uncertainty. Hugging my two children that morning and leaving them was very emotional. I hugged them for Carole, kissed them twice, and promised to give Mummy a kiss and hug from each of them as soon as I saw her. Driving in the sunshine and my own rain, I wondered about what might be on the horizon. Truth be told, it was all a little unnerving.

I stopped at the local store and bought Carole's favourite brunch food – an assortment of chewy sweets and some chocolate brioche – and arrived at the hospital just after eight to give Mummy her two hugs and kisses. I hugged her like her life depended on it. She still had absolutely no idea why she was in hospital and, all things considered, appeared at ease and quietly bemused. We spent all day together and checked in with the folks at home on a regular basis, even though there was very little to report. Just before lunch, Carole was admitted to one of the hospital wards, where tests and observations continued routinely.

We talked at length about her missing twenty-eight minutes over coffee in the hospital café during the afternoon as I recounted every detail of my theatre of horrors. Carole was desperate to understand, to feel my tears as I felt hers. It was the strangest of strange conversations as we sat and cried together holding hands. It was strange because everything was round the wrong way. There we were, two people, just so in-tune with each other, yet struggling to make sense of each other's emotions.

Everything was upside down and back to front. I wasn't ill, and yet I'd suffered emotionally through the unsettling events of Carole's physical trauma. I found this situation difficult to cope with at times. Carole was ill, and yet she struggled to understand the potential significance of her predicament because she simply had no recollection. She was trying so hard to feed off my emotions and began very slowly to register my commentary and my concern.

Carole had a minor but thankfully tangible connection to events via the physical pain from the rip in her tongue. In the cold light of day, her injury looked even worse than I had remembered. Her speech was still a little lispy, and she grimaced occasionally when attempting her usual eloquence. She eventually realised that to bite through her tongue and to inflict a nasty wound without recollection was, in all seriousness, a fairly big deal.

As we chatted, I think I was outwardly displaying the signs of stress and anxiety that I'd naturally expect Carole to exhibit. She kept telling me not to look so worried. Inversely, Carole was the sensitive, caring, and empathetic partner trying to comfort me in her time of need. For a short time, our natural roles seemed to be confused and very oddly mixed up. It was like I was the patient.

Perhaps it was blessing that this was how things were – nature's way of protecting Carole from memories unkind. We each understood, in a sort of safe and bizarre way, the mixed-up topsy-turviness of the other's perspective. Carole was able to learn about herself with a degree of emotional detachment, and with my gentle repetition of events these emotions would eventually find a degree of reattachment. I had to rebuild Carole's memory of her potentially life-threatening event guiding my imagery and my multi-sensory connections to her.

I tried to put myself in her shoes for a moment and wondered what it must feel like to be Carole. It was difficult to find a suitable simile. My only conclusion was without her own memory, it would be impossible for Carole to fully reconnect all her senses to those lost twenty-eight minutes. The best I could really hope for at that point was for her to understand. If she could understand what I saw and felt, then maybe in time she'd be able to connect that back to a pseudo-memory I'd have to implant gradually.

I became aware of the very thin line between giving Carole too much information versus just enough information in order to inspire the right amount of visualisation to invoke her realisation of my senses. What became painful, but beautiful, for me to understand was that despite her fragile condition, Carole was more concerned about me and the children than she was herself. She cried because I was crying, and I cried because she had no idea of how potentially ill she could be. She was just being Carole. She was being unconditional love in that moment. Over coffee that afternoon, I remember thinking she was simply amazing as we sat there together in the really weird place we called our life.

Evening arrived quickly as time slipped by. Time has a habit of doing this when you immerse yourself completely in the company of your perfect companion. Very reluctantly, I left a slightly more anxious Carole at the hospital. All the tests conducted thus far had proved to be inconclusive. On the one hand, this was good, because she'd returned to a natural state of external healthiness for a while. On the other hand, it was obvious that something wasn't quite right, and we needed to find out what was happening.

When I got home, I reassured the children that Mummy was OK but that she'd had a nasty shock that morning, which meant her stay in hospital would be for a little while longer. The children understood that Mummy needed to get the right medicine and care to make her better. Family life that evening was a little different. Perhaps we were being shown a glimpse of the future. I made phone calls to a few concerned friends and kept them updated on the inconclusiveness of our day. I urged them all not to worry and assured them we would relay any changes. Everyone sent love and warmest wishes, which were heartfelt, appreciated, and very comforting.

Walking back into our bedroom for the first time brought everything flooding back. I sat for a while on the end of the bed and was alone again with thoughts haphazardly painting new scenarios but trying to avoid arrival and conclusion. It was difficult to know what to think. I changed the bed linen and finally made it to sleep after twenty-two hours awake. While I slept in a colder and roomier bed than usual, I was oblivious to the actions of the hospital staff during the wee small hours of the following morning.

An unfamiliar breakfast routine was adopted for the second consecutive morning at home. Somehow, the three of us emerged as ready as we could be to face another day of temporary separation and disruption. I dropped the children off again with their grandparents and headed back to the hospital. The sun was shining and the sky was blue as I navigated rush-hour traffic once more. I parked the car and cast off optimistically into the sea of our uncertainty. The water was slightly more temperate that morning, although the waves would become higher and the winds fierce by dusk. A gentle summer breeze accompanied me across the busy car park.

I found Carole wide awake on the ward, which bustled with an industry of compassion and care. She looked more fatigued and a little paler than yesterday, although her eyes retained their sunshine smile. It was lovely to hug her as she asked about the children. I kissed her three times.

I'd only been there a few minutes when the orange nurse popped over to see Carole. As they chatted, I looked at the medical chart that hung at the foot of Carole's iron bed frame next to a bottle of transparent antibacterial hand wash which I'd used minutes earlier. As I read a few sentences from the general notes section, I had another of those moments of deep and painfully reality. It brought me to my senses with immediate quickening. One word stuck out, just one word. It jumped off the page as I collided with it and it with me. I read it several times, understood its significance straight away, and looked at the nurse, who had been observing me quietly as she chatted personably with Carole. The expression on my face must have given me away.

During the next few minutes, the nurse told us about Carole's eventful morning and how there had been some quite worrying moments. It emerged during conversation that Carole had been diagnosed formally with a condition called epilepsy. As we listened, holding each other's hands, we learned that Carole had severe epilepsy. It occurred to me at that time that the actions of our son at home just a few nights ago had actually saved Carole's life. Nature had woken him to call.

Carole and I looked at each other with a sense of relief. They'd found the reason for her episodes of unconsciousness. What we didn't necessarily compute was that we'd find out why Carole had severe epilepsy later that day.

When Carole asked me, 'What's epilepsy?' I shrugged my shoulders and kept my thoughts silent. The nurse let us know that we'd be seen by two of the hospital's resident neurologists that afternoon. They would explain epilepsy in more detail, along with the medication, treatment, and care that Carole needed.

I remember sitting on the end of the hospital bed numb with fear. I felt sick. My temples went icy cold and my spine shivered. Before I arrived that morning, Carole had been given some anti-epileptic medication, and this probably accounted for her drowsiness and appearance of fatigue. According to the nurse, she'd complained of headaches throughout the night and was given pain relief in industrial-strength dosage. After we'd finished chatting with the nurse, I asked Carole what had happened to her during the early hours.

She looked at me with a very blank expression, shrugged her shoulders, and said, 'I haven't got a clue what you guys were just talking about.' I showed her the notes in the folder that hung on a clip at the foot of her hospital bed. She read them several times. Nothing registered. She said humorously 'Are they sure these notes are mine?' I pointed to the patient's name recorded on the sheet of paper. I sensed that Carole was beginning to understand that something was medically wrong. She wrapped her arms around me quite securely and whispered, 'What's happening to me, Bun? Why can't I remember? Why?'

I whispered back, 'I love you,' asked her to be patient, and reassuringly let her know that we would soon find out.

We enjoyed our time together. We always did. Carole was high on her new cocktail of drugs, and this amplified her natural personality for a while. Just to be in each other's company was enough. Carole was exhausted, but she'd found a way, as she always did, to look positively at our situation despite a few more gaps of memory to think about – or not.

Privately, we both understood that there was perhaps some difficult news on the way. The currency of our relationship had always been communication, honesty, and trust, with a limitless number of hugs thrown in for good measure. That day, our mutual exchange rate didn't fluctuate despite the opportunity for imbalance. Love was the scale upon which we balanced all things. There was greater intensity of touch and sensory intelligence between us. Our hugs were closer and more personal than usual. Our kisses lingered longer, and our hands were inseparable under tightest grasp. Our sensory vibrations had become even more harmonised as we read each other and talked very honestly and openly about life and of the most important people in our world – our children. I think Carole's ability to reflect on the information given by the nurse helped her to contextualise my visual theatre, as suddenly everything became much more real to her.

Up until that point, she'd only really had my version of events to reference things back to. For me, it was a huge relief that others' accounts of their visual transactions could now conjure further imagery and sensitivity and make things more real to Carole. I felt her emotions reach out over a sort of invisible bridge that let each of us know that we were in this together. She allowed me to see her vulnerability as she reached out to embrace my inner child. We were always on the same wavelength, but that day it was much more synchronous. Our reversed roles were slowly starting to correct themselves.

We chatted that afternoon at her bedside while she rested and as we walked around the hospital grounds hand in hand. With permission from the ward staff, we were able to wander off as long as we stayed together. The same gentle summer breeze accompanied us throughout the day as we walked, talked, and reflected about life and love together. We had another coffee in the hospital café and just chatted about the children and the scene before us.

To look at Carole, you would never know how very poorly she really was. Apart from some obvious signs of fatigue, she was a picture of perfect health – my vision of loveliness. As for me, an assembly of butterflies had filled my stomach. They were trying to tell me something – something about love. I felt all aflutter for the rest of the day.

Without Carole's knowledge, I'd asked to speak with a member of the neurology team. Dr Yellow and I discussed the probable outcomes while Carole had a short but much needed nap. Dr Yellow was unable to provide much information but did say they'd be rechecking Carole's brain scans that afternoon. I was not entirely sure why, but my abdominal flutter became painfully uncomfortable as it descended to the bowels of my emotions. Whatever the scans revealed was something that we would both have to accept – again, one of those things easy to say but not necessarily easy to do.

Before I ventured back to Carole, I took a slight detour away from the ward and found myself in a long empty corridor. Slumped against its bare white wall, I had so many things racing around my head. I figured that whatever the outcome was to be, it was ultimately down to me to be the glue that held everyone and everything together. *Hundreds of thousands of people must have epilepsy, maybe millions*, I thought. *If other people can live their lives with epilepsy then so can we.* I had no idea what this meant or how we would cope. All I knew in my heart was that it had to be manageable. Carole and I would just make it manageable. We had each other and we had our children, and that was enough. We would have to make way for new things. We would manage.

We'd arranged for the children to pop into the hospital to see Mummy later that afternoon. Carole had missed them so much and became increasingly excited as the clock ticked away to the time of their arrival. This lifted her spirits. Carole had been in some contact with the children via text and the occasional phone call, but to see them both, hug them and kiss them, was all she'd wanted to do since her admission. We had a meeting to get through, though, before they arrived. The neurology team were running slightly late and we waited nervously. We comforted each other with total honesty and talked with a natural openness that bound our togetherness in thoughts spoken and unspoken.

At roughly four o'clock, the ward sister popped her head around the blue-patterned curtain surrounding Carole's bed, still drawn from her earlier nap, and advised that the team was ready to see us.

Carole let out a heavy sigh. We held hands. She looked me directly in the eyes and simply said, 'Let's do this.'

I asked Carole rhetorically if she was OK, and without another word, with tightest grasp, we walked lockstep through the ward to a small dimly lit room where the two neurology professionals, Dr Red and Dr Yellow, were waiting. The ward sister joined us and sat quietly observing the next fifteen minutes of our lives as they played out in suspended animation. We all shook hands and got the introductions out of the way fairly quickly. Carole sat to my right-hand side. Our hands reconnected. The two neurologists sat opposite us. Forthright and matter-of-fact, Carole opened the meeting.

'So let's get to it – what's wrong with me? Tell me everything you know.'

Dr Red did most of the talking. He explained the situation in terms that we could understand. There was no ambiguity. We learned that the medical team looking after Carole had been about to send her home that morning when it was decided that her brain scans merited further scrutiny. An abnormality had been found. This was not immediately obvious, but during a team consultation a formal diagnosis had been agreed upon.

My hand was clammy and our grip tightened just a little. My heart was sinking, my stomach ascended uncomfortably, and a mist filled my eyes. Carole was focused on the information, so focused.

Dr Red talked us through epilepsy, explaining that this was likely to be a secondary condition caused by something else. I watched Carole as she began to absorb the information. She had switched off her emotions temporarily and was running in management mode. The next part of the conversation went something like this.

Dr Red said, 'Carole, we've found something in your head. It's a tumour. It's in the front right lobe of your brain, and we believe this is the cause of your epilepsy. There are many different types of brain tumour, and we believe this one is what's called a glioma. Tumours are graded in terms of their severity on a scale of one to six, and we believe yours is grade two.' He then went on to explain in the broadest terms the characteristics of each grade but focused on the significance of grade two.

Our hands gripped tighter again. Carole was still unflappable and maintained direct eye contact with the senior consultant as he continued to paint the bigger picture and its peripheral consequences. A tear rolled down my cheek. My heart just sank deeper into my chest, and my eyes dropped to explore the textile floor.

He continued, 'Carole, the tumour is what we call dispersed. This means that it's not in one place in your brain but it's in many different places and it's joined together. Carole, imagine a glass of water. Drop two or three drops of blue ink into it, count to three, and then freeze-frame what you see. This gives you an idea of the three dimensional picture we see inside your head. The clear water in the glass is normal brain tissue. Unfortunately, the tumour is inoperable.'

It was the news no one wants to hear. A brain tumour, cancer, was devastating enough, but to find it inoperable was just the most difficult thing in the whole world. Dr Red proceeded to talk about life expectancy. I was in a million pieces but fought hard to retain my composure because my wife needed me, perhaps more than she had ever needed anyone in her life. I also needed her.

All sorts of things raced at light speed through my head. I found myself shrinking inwardly, diminishing at a molecular level. I wanted to vomit. I thought at one point that I would. The room was no longer in focus. I felt cold. My eyes felt like they were puffy and swollen. My wife just gripped my hand so hard for a few seconds, bringing me back to the room.

Carole must have picked up a micro-signal through our grasp, a twitch or involuntary pulse or something that just told her I was temporarily absent. Perhaps this was just a feeling of intuition as she stood atop our sensory bridge. Sometimes we would say what the other was thinking or we would say the same things at the same time, not just words but often full sentences. Sometimes we even shared the same sleeping dreams. We'd been lucky enough to live out our dreams together as a family. Was I dreaming? I wished I was. All I could think about was Carole and the children.

Carole's reaction to whatever it was that she sensed about me was her way of saying very simply, 'Stay with me.'

I gripped back to acknowledge her, as if to say, 'I am here. I love you.'

We communicated these messages without a glance. I couldn't look at her. I would have gone to pieces right there and then. She let go of my hand.

Carole asked a few questions and we both played back our verbal understanding. Above all else, Carole needed to know just one thing. She'd read my mind.

Very calmly and with the courage and heart of a lion, she simply asked, 'Am I going to orphan my children by Christmas?' She said this without a hint of quiver, anxiousness, sadness, pain, or anything that would give away what she was actually feeling inside. I glanced sideways at her and felt everything swim across her emotional tide as she waited for his answer. She was still and focused. It was calm and peaceful.

With an air of hesitation, Dr Red simply replied, 'It is unlikely, Carole.' The conversation lasted a few more minutes while we tried to ascertain the absolute certainty of the diagnosis. It was absolute. Life expectancy was guesstimated at between five and seven years. Seven years was best-case. Realistically, five years was hopeful on the basis that regular MRI scans would pick up any change to the inoperable sticky pancake growing inside her head. It was explained that any growth of the glioma could be eased with early chemotherapy, radiation therapy, and drug therapy. These were treatments, not cures. Anything below five years was considered unlucky.

The amount of time that the tumour had existed in Carole's brain could not be determined with any accuracy. Predictive discussion was strictly off limits, and the answer 'We just don't know' was given in all cases. The next steps were established in their broadest sense in terms of health care and the likely impact to Carole's quality of life. I sat quietly. I was just about capable of absorbing and processing the news while thinking all the time about Carole and the children, Carole's world and our little family.

We understood the initial approach to drug therapy, the effects of drugs, the range of drugs available, and the trial-and-error method of finding the right combinations to optimise relief. We learned that episodes of unconsciousness were called *seizures*. The type of seizures Carole had experienced were called *tonic-clonic seizures*. People with severe epilepsy suffer this type. General health indicators were explained and observational guidelines given. We understood the possible symptoms and the signs of progressive decline, what to do, and who to contact in the event that Carole's health worsened.

Carole was also advised that with immediate effect she was no longer permitted to drive by law. This was the final blow. Carole thrived on the independence her car provided.

The conversation with the neurology team finished, and we were exhausted. The ward sister, still quietly observing events in the room as they unfolded, was silent. She'd retained the same look on her face as she did when the meeting started. It was one of hope and sadness. She had a gentle and compassionate smile. I marvelled at the courage of these extraordinary professionals who put themselves through the daily rigour of trying to care as best they can in the face of adversity and uncertainty.

Carole and I thanked everyone. We were assured that specialist teams would be there to support Carole in every way. They were also there to support me and our children. We were offered family counselling and various other measures but quietly declined them. We needed time to absorb, digest, process, and really understand what we'd just been told.

To be completely honest, I was beside myself. No words can describe the emotion and intensity and depth of feeling. Our world had collapsed in a moment. Everything imaginable had changed in the blink of an eye, in a heartbeat. Carole was literally on borrowed time, and no one knew how much. My head was spinning, and it hurt. Carole was beginning a journey with only one outcome and one destination.

Then it hit me: Carole was dying. My lovely, lovely wife was dying. I knew her so well and yet couldn't begin to imagine what she must have been going through as she felt her long-term future and the prospect of old age evaporate into thin air. I sensed her heart begin to break silently. She was beautiful.

Right there in that instant, I understood something quite profound. Perhaps the purpose of my journey through life thus far had been a simple one. Perhaps it was one of preparation. Perhaps it was preparation to live in a moment, to live in this moment. Maybe it was more than purpose. Maybe it was about care, roles, and responsibilities. It was about emotions and senses. It was about life. It was about love. It was about the most powerful and beautiful kind that was Carole's love.

Was this another moment that joined some dots? Whatever it was, it hurt like hell. Carole was hurting, and I hurt with her and for her and for our little family. It felt like all these things were somehow connected to time and its relative dimension is space and bonded tightly to a single moment of consciousness. I needed to somehow find the ability to support Carole. What to say or do? I had no idea where to start. I didn't really get the enormity of the task in front of us, but then how could I? I understood the purpose but not the path.

Carole, however, understood. In a way I find difficult to explain, it was as if Carole understood everything and everything was absolute. She knew all that was and was to be. She had been calm within her thoughtfulness. It was peaceful.

We escaped the ward. Walking the corridor, we decided to grab another coffee in the café to talk through the seriousness of our future, our immediate priorities, our children. I held her hand and turned to face her. Carole's eyes were glazed over, and she began to shake gently from head to toe as she tried to cope with the adrenaline surge that she'd somehow managed to suppress until then. We were eye to eye, cheek to cheek, and then nose to nose.

Exploring her facial features, I said nothing for a few seconds. I simply cupped my wife's face with both hands, whispered 'I love you,' and kissed her so gently through our mist. Carole buried her head in my shoulder and whispered back my nickname softly three times in my ear.

She whispered gently, 'I don't want to die, Bun, I don't want to die. Why me?'

We were inseparable, we always were, and somehow in a place of our own we knew that we always would be. We stood alone, together, as one immovable force, with clenched embrace and in complete symbiosis. We cried and buckled into each other's arms. I stroked the back of her head and felt her tears through my shirt. She was as fragile and as beautiful as a snowflake. She was roaring at life on the inside. Her heart was melting, and all I could do in that moment was feel and respond to her. I wanted that moment to last forever. I still do.

On our way down the rest of the corridor, holding hands and wiping faces, something happened. It was something that I will treasure for eternity and a day. It was poetry in suspended motion. It was love.

Never did I ever expect to witness the most moving transformation of anyone in the history of my life. It was just as if an invisible magic wand cast ethereal incantation prompting Carole to search deep within herself to find an innate inner strength. From where or how she summoned this strength, I may never know. She stopped walking, turned to face me, and held both my hands at waist level. She looked into my eyes through her own watery abyss and then she spoke. Carole spoke to me with what could only be her soul.

She simply whispered, 'It could be worse, much worse, Adrian.'

I looked at her with a puzzled pause. I was about to speak and then subconsciously realised that she'd called me Adrian. Carole never called me Adrian.

A calm, soft, but assured female voice inside my head literally whispered, 'Listen.'

Carole's voice quivered as her body trembled through her tears. 'This could be happening to one of our children,' she said.

I cry an ocean every time I think of that moment. The penny had dropped.

'We'll be all right, Bun, we'll be all right. We've got each other. We'll get through this – we have to.'

We stared lovingly into each other's eyes in a moment that seemed to last forever. In that moment, I began to understand a little more about love, allowing my butterflies of earlier to fly freely upon each tear and within each aching pulse of heart. I can tell you that it was beautiful. I can tell you that it hurt. Through her own pain and her pain for me and our children, Carole found something I can't necessarily explain. It was as if she'd acknowledged that the only thing in the world that she would be prepared to die for was love. Carole showed me that to love and be loved unconditionally, you first have to become that which you offer to others.

We sobbed on each other's shoulder and let our hearts speak honestly. I never wanted to remove my arms from around Carole's shaking but beautiful frame. A little piece of both of us died there and then in the corridor that day. It was replaced by something else. Carole's words have stayed with me. These are the words that make tingle the top of my nose and release a stream about my face which now rests upon the shoulder of my own inner butterfly.

If there is ever a metaphorical moment in life when an angel's wings unfold to reveal the soul, colossal beauty, and true inner strength of someone during the most extreme and cruellest of circumstances, this was the moment. Carole's wings simply unfolded as she calmly surrendered to, acknowledged, and embraced her level crossing. Carole had accepted what was happening to her. Through Carole's love and what I can only describe as her selflessness, I had also accepted it. I was kicking and screaming on the inside, but accepting nonetheless. What else could I do? What could we do? She had breached a mortal boundary and understood in just a few seconds more than I could ever comprehend in my lifetime to that point. In a single moment of her inner beauty, I'd felt the flutter of her deepest emotions.

As my life with Carole had itself unfolded, I'd been able to piece together a picture postcard of knowledge and wonder that gave me endless appreciation, day after day, of the magnificence of this lovely lady. A lady I was simply honoured to call my wife, my best friend, and my soulmate. As another friend would remind some years later, 'She was the toughest lady I ever met.'

On our walk to the café, Carole and I managed to put perspective around everything in a rational, calm, pragmatic, and determined way. She was simply breath-taking when only minutes earlier, her breath had been momentarily taken away. Only minutes earlier, she was told that her future was certain but uncertain, her life expectancy slashed. She would most likely predecease her parents, her husband, and her children. In all probability, within the next five years or maybe less she was going to die.

It was as if the bond that had united us so perfectly throughout many years of happy marriage had been cemented by an unknown force so powerful that our collective understanding of everything and each other was all that we would ever need to see us through the rest of her life. This was a bond of nothing more and nothing less than something I can only ever describe in the simplest of terms as love. This bond was so strong that it would be my strength within when all without had potential for chaos. We were determined that no matter the consequences, we would begin to live the rest of our lives like every day was the last day, like every meal was the last meal, every hug the last hug, and every kiss the last. We'd lived our lives together with this philosophy always, only now it had a more mortal and meaningful significance.

As we walked just holding hands, we attracted some strange looks. It was probably the piggy eyes and red noses. Carole's inner beacon, that little spark of light in her heart, radiated more powerfully and more beautifully than ever before. It was intense. I felt it. She glowed on the inside, and maybe her energy was now on display for everyone to feel and to see. Maybe they could see her wings.

Coffee under grasp, we found a table and began to talk about receiving our two little visitors in shortening time. It was another difficult conversation. It ripped us both apart, but we had no choice but to approach the wind head-on and maintain a steady course to our horizon of many unseen sunsets. With pragmatism, based on our ideal of doing the right thing because it was always the right thing to do, we talked through the difficulties. What would we tell the children? Should we tell them? When could we tell them and how did we do this? In a very controlled way, through what on the surface seemed to be an impossible task, we reached a decision quickly, sensibly, and with absolute togetherness.

The decision was easy. Its delivery, however, was something that needed very delicate consideration and a pair of super-safe hands. Carole looked up from where she was staring in thoughtful silence. With a wiping of her brow with both hands from the centre outwards, and with the heaviest of heavy hearts, she sighed and then spoke as a mother.

'We have to tell them. We tell them everything. We owe them this much. I owe them this much. I am their Mummy.'

Carole sobbed quietly, and so I held the hand of love. She streamed my fears and I wiped her face. Her head dropped again to my shoulder, and my shirt absorbed another patch of love's purest stream. There was a moment of beauty and real heartache as Carole searched her soul for the hardest answer that somehow she already knew. There was no internal struggle with her conscience but more a calm and incredibly emotionally honest surrender.

Sometimes in life, there are no words powerful enough to properly convey what you feel, hear, share, or see. This was one of those moments. We would tell the children together that evening at home. We would find a language they would understand but would not be afraid of a language that was clear and not complicated. It would be a language of honesty born only of compassion and love's eternal embrace. We agreed in that instant that we would never hide anything from them.

Carole and I were beginning to think about the path that we would take now as a family. Everything was changing. There were new things that we would be forced to consider for the first time and make sense of. There was so much to think about that potential existed to be overwhelmed to a point of paralysis and joint seizure. Ever mindful of the need to embrace change, we also recognised that going forward was about keeping life as normal as possible for the children. For the short term, we decided that a 'one day at a time' approach was needed to soften the impact of forced lifestyle transformation. I took on the unspoken responsibility of managing the children's expectations of the most difficult outcome of our world of difference.

To go forward as a cohesive unit, given the relativity of Carole's life expectancy, it was important that full transparency regarding her condition was maintained between the four of us throughout. Carole and I were already defining the new normal that was quickly becoming our life. Over a time frame of less than sixty minutes, we had moved through almost every conceivable emotion. We'd contemplated, understood, and accepted perhaps the second worst possible life scenario and made one of the hardest decisions together. I struggle to find the words to tell you how much I loved Carole that day and for every day of our life together and beyond. Perhaps love is the only word that requires no explanation, no proliferation or metaphor when understood and experienced unconditionally in her most beautifully feminine form.

Our lives were about to change in ways unthinkable and unimaginable. Change was already upon us. It was just the beginning. A few days ago, we were all happy-go-lucky, without a care in the world. Three days later, the artist of our humanity was painting a uniquely different picture. There was new purpose, new direction, and a profoundly greater emphasis on the beauty and fragility of life and of everything. There was challenge and opportunity. It was the beginning of a journey with a perspective of difference.

A new chapter had started, but nothing was ending. As we turned each leaf, we hadn't realised that we'd started to evolve with the characters that animated the pages of our emotions. These were the characters who tugged at the strings of the music of life and found strength and understanding at times when nothing made much sense. We had stopped being and so started to begin.

Carole and I knew we would have to be rational. We would have to continue to be each other's conscience. We were always the devoted other and the voice inside each other's heads. We were the calm in the storm and the voice of reason when no reason could be found. Carole had always been the sense in my nonsense and the sense in our sensitivities. The real in our reality had arrived unexpectedly, like the most magnificent thunderstorm descending unexpectedly on a day of brilliant sunshine. It cast darkest clouds, vertical rain, and a super-charged bolt of lightning that brought natural wonder, danger, and devastation, and then eventually a restoration of calm and balance. Our children were Carole's sunshine, illness was our rain, and Carole was our super-charged lightning bolt. Together, in the café, we emerged calmly and as best we could to be each other's rainbow.

As we finished our coffees, Carole quickly attended to her piggy and blackened eyes, which had rendered her temporarily Goth-like. I think secretly Carole always wanted to be a Goth! Her eyes had recovered sufficiently to restore their unmistakable sparkle. That afternoon, her smooth, usually pale freckly skin found a new tone that glowed of summer's roses. It highlighted her natural beauty and the softness of her features in a way I'd never noticed before. Carole's bright eyes, the windows to her soul, were the rarest and most wonderful colour of hazel brown that somehow, in a moment, illuminated that which released the art of her inner peace. She allowed me to see through these windows every day, willingly sharing her thoughts and feelings.

Carole had perfected the art of excess mascara removal by running simultaneously her second finger on each hand along her lower eyelids, wiping horizontally in the direction of nose to ear. She applied this craft now and used me as her invisible mirror to check her make-up. She asked, 'Do I look all right, Bun?' waving her hands with wing-like motion to calm herself and dry her fingers.

I simply replied 'You look beautiful!' I sat mesmerised in the company of love as she smiled and sniffed her way back to sparkle.

Carole's folks arrived at the café with our little ones. With an injection of immediate happiness, Carole exclaimed, 'Hello, babbas!' *Babbas* was the colloquial term she used for her babies. The children were as excited as Carole was. Everyone exchanged hugs, squeezes, and kisses as Carole battled to hide her emotions. She dug deep to keep everything as normal as possible.

Over coffee, Carole and I had talked about what we needed to do when the children arrived, and both of us were now switching from our emotional state of mind to one full of purpose and sharp objective. Carole had been steadfast in her need to tell her folks personally, and as soon as possible, about her diagnosis and prognosis. Naturally, Carole had rejected my offer to do this for her. While she did this, my job was to distract the children in the hospital shop with an offer of sweets, chocolate, ice-cream, or whatever else they might want. Carole simply explained that Mummy had to talk to Nanny and Granddad very quickly and that Daddy would take them to the shop to get goodies.

Carole guided her Mum and Dad to the outside area of the café, where they found seats at an empty table in the sunshine. I observed the three of them for a few moving seconds as Carole delivered her news. I battled with my emotions in that moment, with my two little ones at my side waiting patiently to be taken the few yards to the shop. Carole didn't beat about the bush; she was controlled and strong, and I knew in just a few seconds that the news every parent dreads had been dispatched matter-of-factly. They were facing the scenario that Carole was herself grateful to be avoiding. The facial expressions of her parents changed in the blink of an eye, and their eyes dropped to explore the flagstone floor.

I wanted to be with her but respected her need for privacy and her resolute need to do this her way, Carole's way. Besides, my job was equally important. I love chocolate.

I followed Carole's jaw-droppingly inspirational lead and put my emotions away in a locked drawer for just a little while. As we walked to the shop, the children were blissfully unaware of the issues of the day and the news they would be hearing that evening. It was difficult to make sense of anything. I had an odd feeling that perhaps everyone in the hospital at that very moment had a similar story to tell, a similar experience, some perhaps more devastating than others – some happy stories and some second chances.

We'd been given a second chance that day. Carole was still living, breathing, feeling, doing, and managing. Despite the rocky road ahead, the fact that we had this opportunity, for however long it lasted, was all that mattered. Perhaps everyone present in that moment was supposed to be in that place at that time for a reason. The short walk to the shop brought a revelation of sorts. Chocolate never tasted so good.

4

Through the Nightmares

arole and I journeyed back from the hospital together shortly after we'd collected a large quantity of prescription medication from the on-site pharmacy. On the way back to the car, we joked about taking on the appearance of two shifty-looking puffy-eyed individuals walking through the hospital with a very large bag of premium-grade psychoactive substances. We were slightly gobsmacked at the number and frequency of different medications that Carole needed. It was just a bit weird – funny weird and, well, just plain weird. The children had already gone on ahead with their grandparents, and we'd arranged to rendezvous at our house within the hour.

As the sun began its slow descent, we talked in the car about the landmarks that obscured our horizon. Carole had let her folks know that she was terminally ill and had outlined what this meant to her. We'd have to work out what this meant to us as a family as we grew into our collective funny weird. We talked and cried and talked and cried some more on the way home as time quickened upon us to break some difficult news to the most special people in Carole's heart.

Carole was recovering from three days of extreme personal challenge and was physically, emotionally, and mentally exhausted. Even though she was knackered, she looked great once the piggy-eyes had dried. I was as concerned for her as she was for me, and since she'd insisted on telling her Mum and Dad herself, I asked if I could take the lead on talking to the kids. I thought that maybe she'd find comfort if I did the talking, just in case the situation was a tad overwhelming. I probably don't have to tell you that my request was gently denied, and I need not have worried. Carole repeated the words from our conversation in the hospital café earlier that afternoon.

'I am their Mummy. I owe them this much.'

We talked briefly about wording and how to put things in perspective in a soft and direct way without fear.

Carole smiled through her emotions in the car, assuring me, 'I know what to say.'

She returned momentarily to her Goth-like face as she contemplated the reality of what she was about to do. What was left of her mascara ran silently down her cheeks before being wiped away once more with symmetrical precision.

We arrived home, had a huge hug, and made sure we looked OK before venturing again into unknown territory. All sorts of things had gone through our minds in the car – all the what-ifs, whys, and wherefores. It was difficult to know what to expect during our next passage of time. The house welcomed back its Lady after an absence of three very long days with the scents of peaceful vanilla. Whispa sidled up to Carole and purred around her ankles in the hall.

'It feels good to be home,' she said. 'I'm dying for a decent cup-o-coffee. Stick the kettle on, Bun! Now, where are my babbas?'

There was a spring in Carole's voice as it jumped to a playful and childlike tone very naturally. In the lounge, the children greeted Mummy with kisses and squishy hugs before settling on the sofas. She told them again how much she'd missed them. The three best friends talked for a few minutes about what Mummy had been up to in hospital before she said calmly, 'I've got something to tell you both when Daddy's made coffee.'

Right on cue, coffee was ready. There was no anxiety, no hesitation or hint of reluctance on anyone's part. The children sat next to each other on one sofa while Carole sat opposite them on the other. I sat on the floor next to Carole, and then she began.

'So, the doctors at the hospital have found out what's wrong with me. I've got something called epilepsy. Epilepsy makes my brain fuzzy – it makes it tickle, and when it tickles then I have what they call a seizure. A seizure is like when my brain has forgotten what to do.' There were a few questions and answers that followed, and then Carole got to the other thing she wanted to say. 'The doctors also know what causes my epilepsy.' There was a short pause. 'It's because there is something in my head that won't ever go away, and that's called a tumour.'

One of the children asked, 'Does that mean you're going to die?' My heart was already in a few more pieces by this point, and I wasn't sure if I could've answered that question without bursting into tears.

Carole just carried on, matter-of-fact, no deviation in her voice, which was still bouncing and jumping around. 'Yes, that means I'm going to die.' There was another short pause of composure. 'Everyone dies one day,' she said. 'Most people don't know when they're going to die – but I sort of do. The doctors said it won't be for about five years, so we don't have to worry about all that now.'

There were a few more questions before Carole asked me if she'd left anything out. I let them know that Mummy had to take some tablets every day and that Mummy might have some seizures before her tablets stopped them. The tablets might make Mummy very tired and a bit forgetful, and that was all perfectly normal.

I finished by saying that 'if Mummy has a seizure, all you need to do is come and get me or just shout "Dad!" and I will look after Mummy.'

'Right' Carole said. 'Let's have a cuddle!'

And so they did. In the blink of an eye, family life had returned to some degree of normality. Carole put her slippers and PJs on, unpacked her bag, and devoted the rest of the evening to the children. Carole was never without her slippers! Our world was a little better for the time being, albeit very different on many levels. Without realising, we were beginning a sort of new normality together, and we were all grateful for the opportunity.

That evening, after the kids had gone to sleep, the two of us sat on the sofa and played back the last few days. It was a little easier to put things in perspective, and Carole was beginning to absorb the magnitude of the potential challenges ahead. We were all just so happy to have her back at home.

She was still unable to remember the tonic-clonic episodes that had put her life in grave danger. The pain from the rip in her tongue would be a constant reminder that not all was well as it healed over the next week or so. I had some idea what epilepsy really looked like at its worst but understood little about epilepsy in its everyday form. We'd picked up some literature from the hospital which outlined in very simple terms the various degrees of severity, how to identify this, and what to do in the event that a seizure occurs.

We were told by the neurology team that we should think about epilepsy and the brain tumour as two different conditions for treatment purposes. It took a while to get our heads around this – especially as one was the root cause of the other. Trawling through the information was exhausting for both of us. Lots to take in, absorb, understand, process, and evaluate. Before we retired to the comfort of sleep, we decided there and then that it was important to look at the short- to medium-term milestones that awaited us as a family and as individuals. Being in the presence of the children had lifted Carole above the obvious mental turmoil of coming to terms with so many things. Her industrial-strength medication began to relax her as she found a lofty mellow edge at a time when her thinking also needed a little elevation.

As I sat with my space cadet, we penned a few simple goals for the next five years. Five years, we agreed, was best-case. Five years very quickly became our 'ideal world' scenario. What hit Carole like an express train was that she'd most likely miss out on so many life events that parents would naturally expect to share with their children. This broke her heart, and no drug could stop it.

We shared the energy of a strong and silent hug, which prompted shoulders full of tears to glue us ever more tightly together. Carole overlooked her heartache for the remainder of our conversation to focus on understanding the bigger picture. I don't know how she did this, but it helped us to put a little list of events down on paper.

In five years' time, it would be August 2014, and Carole would be nearing her forty-fifth birthday. I would be 46. In five years' time, the children would be 15 and 18 respectively. Their weddings didn't feature on our list, nor did twenty-first birthdays or grandchildren. Carole had also wanted to add to our family numbers, and we'd previously talked quite openly about having another baby. We touched on this point only briefly as the reality of recent events took tighter grasp.

I couldn't write most of the other mini-milestones down here on this page, even though I think about them every day. We'd always dreamed of growing old together, a house full of cats, and a bus full of children. The house of our dreams was a white windmill or a picture-perfect cottage with thatched roof and a tall butterfly meadow of wild flowers and pollen scents. I'd always wished that maybe one day we'd retire to a lighthouse together and pen a novel or two, looking out into a limitless ocean of possibilities where imagination, tranquillity, and love ruled the waves. These dreams evaporated into thin air on the sofa, as did many more.

It was late when Carole simply said, 'I know this stuff will probably kill me one day, but I'm not gonna let it stop me living my life.'

We stood together, clenched in an embrace in the hallway at the bottom of the stairs. I stared into her eyes, and in that moment we found something I was unable to explain at the time. Carole checked on the kids, as she always did, before climbing into freshly fragranced bed linens for the first time in three days. She cried herself to sleep in my arms as I stroked the wispy feathered-down hairline above her brow. Even though I could not sleep, it was a night of a thousand dreams.

* * *

Carole and the children had been off school for the summer holidays, and I'd taken short-notice leave from work to be with Carole in hospital. We'd been looking forward to our annual family holiday booked for the third week in August. On medical grounds, we'd sort of encouraged each other that we shouldn't take the holiday for lots of reasons – mainly common-sense ones. Even though this sat awkwardly with us, because it poured more change onto family plans, we eventually cancelled our holiday after negotiating a distasteful process of phone calls, correspondence, and expense to prove that Carole was indeed dying. Carole was distraught, because it meant that the children were affected, and privately she blamed herself for this. In time, she would reach a difficult but reconcilable understanding of self-forgiveness.

Over the next few weeks, the initial disruptions to routines began to slip silently into a new framework of life. It was OK, and Carole and I worked hard to think, speak, and act in a thoughtful way that allowed the children soft transition to this framework. Epilepsy had become our new house guest, and it showed no signs of wanting to leave anytime soon.

Carole's drugs were so strong that it wasn't possible to jump straight to a high dosage to accelerate Carole's seizure control. Meds were introduced slowly on a sort of 'build-up' programme, and therefore seizures were inevitable over the next eight weeks. That said, even the smallest doses knocked Carole off her feet very quickly. The most potent tablet was taken at night-time, just before midnight, so that Carole could begin to recuperate through seizure-free sleep. This drug was so powerful we called it the 'elephant drug', as it would've knocked out an elephant or a herd of elephants very quickly!

A drug chart was made and stuck to one of the cupboard doors in the kitchen, with colour coding for each different tablet. Carole had decided some years before to resume birth-control medication, so we included this cycle in the chart too. We weren't sure that Carole would always remember to take her tablets, so things were put in place to help. Alarms on phones and clocks were set at different times throughout the day to remind us to remind Carole to take her medication. I'd often text her at drug time if either of us was out and about running errands or walking to the shops. It didn't take long to get used to the new sounds echoing around the house or the activities that soon became routine.

The drugs made Carole a little irritable sometimes; they invoked almost instant fatigue, and we began to see some changes to her physical health. Skin rashes appeared almost overnight. She had problems with her eyesight, and there were facial tics and minor infections. Carole also began to lose weight. It was difficult to ascertain any direct connection between the introduction of new powerful tablets for new health issues, but the implications of change were clearly visible. This visibility enabled us to place things under a degree of management and analytical observation.

Her mental health remained more or less intact, apart from the obvious conflicts with her inner self. It was difficult for Carole to avoid the stress of beginning to live with terminal illness, but we very quickly adopted a simple approach to stress management.

As long as we continued to talk, which we did, we realised that the causes of stress were the triggers for one of two actions. Firstly, if we could alleviate the thing causing stress, the stress would go away through resolution. Secondly, if we couldn't affect the cause of stress positively, we stopped stressing and instead accepted it through a concerted effort to change thought processes. Either way, we were reducing the stress levels of a quite stressful situation. I guess we'd always done this together but had never really stopped to appreciate it for its real value.

Illness had forced us to stop and evaluate a whole raft of things, and it was a real eye-opener. Carole was acutely aware of the changes to our lives as a family, and as they unfolded, she began to accept, adapt, and reason with what she could see, feel, and know. As Carole learned, so she taught.

Carole began to experience different types of seizures. The children and I shared in these experiences visually and emotionally. It changed our priorities and routines, our individual thought processes, our understanding of each other, our sensitivities, and ultimately the world in which we lived. It changed everything. The four of us made a commitment that we would always talk honestly, be open about our feelings, and never hide anything from each other, no matter how bad things got. Carole and I explained to the children that our friendship with each other was so important. It was the most important thing, as this would help us get through anything together.

Without necessarily being aware, Carole and I found ourselves on a sort of accelerated life path. By this I mean that our family dynamic had been propelled thirty or forty years into the future by illness, and yet we didn't necessarily have those extra years of life experience and wisdom to help us cope with the speed of this dynamic propulsion. On the surface, this should have caused unease and complication. The very skills we needed or thought we needed had been denied to us by time. Carole and I were lucky to an extent because we always worked stuff out together. Our natural affinity with each other, even though it would be tested time and time again, was actually the map that guided us through the ups and downs and the bumps in the road. Together, Carole and I knew that there was nothing that could derail our resolve.

We thought that maybe all of the challenges we faced on our winding and bumpy road into the future were in some way keys.

They were perhaps the keys to unlocking the missing blocks of wisdom and life skills that time had denied us. With each bump, our knowledge would be accelerated to prepare us for the next hurdle, brick wall, or challenge. All we had to do was recognise this, adapt, and learn.

We began to look at life in a completely different way. What was always difficult to accept – maybe not just accept but understand – was that Carole and I were better placed to manage and cope because we were in our late thirties and early forties. The children, on the other hand, were also being propelled at light speed without those extra years of experience, and yet they were beginning to adapt as well. It was as if their lost years were not lost but perfectly understood. Perhaps, as they were already in the season of their own learning and development, they found a natural capacity to flex and respond to change. After all, this is what all children do.

They didn't have the rigidity and confinement of structure or culture either. It was almost as though the children knew how to manage their fear far better than we did as adults. Perhaps this was a kind of blessing; they'd had little exposure to regressive social ideology, and this helped to positively centre their thinking and behaviour. Whatever it was, to their absolute credit, both children were taking a positive approach to some not-so-nice things. This was hard to watch, and it shredded Carole's heart a little more with each passing day.

It was Carole's awareness of the little things that were changing in life that helped her adapt to the bigger picture and its peripheral landscapes. Little things like her use of language – saying something in a different way so as not to shock or injure but to teach through a gentle transfer of action and vision accompanied by soft words. She wouldn't necessarily tell us what to do but showed us with her unique altruistic adaptations in the face of a problem – like checking her motor skills, seeking new memory techniques, or finding alternative methods to preparing food. I think it was this inner temporal shift in her attitude toward illness, and ultimately toward herself, that turned her thinking on its head and enabled her to look within with more conviction to simply be.

As we set and reset our expectations as a family, so we began the process of learning about our new lives together. We were all learning about ourselves and each other through a natural process. Carole and I were slowly teaching the children positively about many things, and the children, in return, were teaching us. Their acceptance and understanding, as well as their ability to cope, showed us that we could all traverse the bumps in the road as long as we were honest and just talked to each other. This had always been at the core of our modus operandi, and circumstances had elevated it to a position of greater awareness and understanding. We weren't necessarily doing anything new or innovative, just trying as best we could to manage the effects of negative change in a positive way.

We began to witness first-hand the destructive forces of epilepsy. The literature from the hospital covered the basics and was initially the guide we used to unravel the traumas of our shared visual theatre. Not only were seizures becoming a part of life, but we'd noticed they were a little mischievous too. In the early weeks following diagnosis, seizures would creep up on Carole unexpectedly and play games with her psyche, almost as if to say, 'This is what I am, and as you begin to know me, you can learn and apply knowledge and substance into temporary care.'

Each time Carole had a seizure, we all learned something, and we talked quite openly of the shared experience. We were learning to check when the last lot of meds had been taken or if there was a pattern emerging with regard to duration or time of day. I started looking for some of the things that might've sparked the seizure into life in the hope that we could identify, manage, and then avoid it. For me personally, it was terribly difficult watching the love of my life go through pain and suffering time and time and time again. It was always Carole's resolve that softened my own trauma. It repeatedly broke my heart.

Apart from the tonic-clonic seizures – the most severe kind – there were complex partial seizures, simple partial seizures, and a few other vapour-like or epigastric sensations emanating in her stomach. Carole described the vapours as 'wispy' and having toxic or acrid tastes and smells. She compared the wispiness to the swimming-fish-like sensations she'd experienced in the womb during the early stages of her pregnancies.

Carole loved each of her pregnancies passionately, and she used to say 'being pregnant was like being in love with love.'

I would tell her that 'to see you in bloom with our child is the most beautiful thing I've ever seen.'

In a funny sort of way, the epigastric sensations reminded Carole of her love for her unborn babies. This sensory treasure of memory, profound and as moving as it was, prompted Carole to tell me one day, 'Sometimes epilepsy is a comfort to me – it's not all bad.'

The complex partial seizures, on the other hand, were something different and quite difficult to witness. They were unpleasant for Carole to experience, as they made her feel physically sick, and she'd often take on a very inhuman appearance. There were good days and bad days and prolonged periods of rest and recuperation mixed with the occasional nightmare of incessant illness. From one day to the next, we were never quite sure what to expect.

Over one four-day period, Carole had a total of fifty-five seizures. Twenty-eight of these were complex partial and one was tonic-clonic, while the remaining twenty-six were simple. The tonic-clonic event lasted over thirty minutes, during which time Carole was unconscious and unresponsive. It took me back to the horror of Carole's missing twenty-eight minutes – as if I needed reminding of how beautiful and fragile the gift of life is. I have no idea how her physical body withstood the relentless barrage of debilitating attacks, but it did. Carole's mental toughness often left me struggling for words in the same way she struggled for breath. She was breath-taking.

With every complex partial seizure, Carole would become absent of mind. This dense foggy state would descend instantly out of nowhere and take charge. There were no real obvious signs to let us know Carole was beginning to enter a state of seizure, although once this had started, it didn't take long to know that help was needed. Regardless of where she was or what she was doing, disorientation took firm grip. She would stare into space and be unresponsive to the physical world around her. This was the only real indicator that her brain was feeling ticklish.

In just seconds, Carole would have no control of her facial muscles as they quickly distorted and remoulded her features beyond our normal recognition. The elasticity of her usually tight and unblemished freckly skin disappeared. The outer construction of her face morphed into a version of one of Edvard Munch's four expressionist paintings referred to collectively as 'Der Schrei der Natur' – the Scream of Nature. Her mouth and eyelids drooped. She'd blink uncontrollably while struggling to maintain her centre of gravity. Her saliva gland went into spontaneous overdrive, causing her to dribble uncontrollably.

Speech was always lost as she battled breathlessly to communicate. Communication in all its forms was impossible. Her disorientation was both physical and intracranial, causing a complete loss of the coordination of brain and body and the usual cognisance between. It was as though her soul had left her temporarily. Mid-seizure, she was left looking like an empty shell of bone and tissue that struggled to find form or to perform at a basic level – alone and lost between two worlds. Her brain switched everything off to prevent recognition of imagery and emotions, but perhaps most importantly to block memory. Watching her, we realised that she was powerless to stop the horrible effects of the seizure. We were as powerless as Carole was, but we always had memory.

Carole, without comprehension and with little control, would vigorously wipe her eyes and rub her face in a desperate attempt to resolve something that she intuitively knew was happening. The movement of her hands to her eyes showed me that she was aware of the uncharacteristic blinking and distortion of sight. During the seizure, Carole's vision was severely impaired, to the extent that she may have been temporarily blind. The constant and rough wiping of her face looked like she was trying to push back her skin as she sensed it was collapsing about its form.

Carole had a natural instinct to wander and walk off with only crude knowledge of her surroundings. She was attracted to windows and external doors as though she was searching for light or sunshine. If she was ever seated at the start of a seizure, she'd just get up without warning, and we'd have to let her wander of her own free will. As she walked in her scream, one hand would be outstretched in front of her while the other attempted repairs to her temporary mask. When these things happened, they happened all at the same time.

If you were in close proximity to Carole, it was easy to see that she found breathing very difficult. This was probably due to the drowning sensation caused by excessive saliva production and the body's instinctive reaction to swallow. She fought for every gasp of air. It was important that Carole's movements remain unrestricted so that the severity of seizure didn't escalate to a state of unconsciousness.

Complex partials had durations of between twenty or thirty seconds to three or four minutes – sometimes longer. They didn't care where she was, what she was doing, or who she was with, and they had no respect for Carole's safety. Not to underestimate the physical trauma Carole experienced during moments of kafuffled complexity, to see this first-hand was terrifying and horrific. It was terrifying because I was powerless. The only thing I could do was redirect Carole away from danger with absolute minimum contact. It was horrific because her face changed beyond recognition.

I always talked to Carole during her seizures although, as with her eyesight, her hearing was almost non-existent. Nevertheless, talking to her slowly and with few but purposeful words helped her during the recovery process. When beginning recovery, she could hear just a little and would show reaction to sound through head movement or a change of her direction of travel – usually towards a noise or a light source.

Recovery was the end of a seizure and the beginning of her body's auto-responsive jump-start, a sort of chemical and electrical reboot of her brain that reprogrammed her body back to a state of natural beauty and biology. As Carole's scream retreated silently to its invisible hiding place, giving reprieve until its next incarnation, it was possible to hear the blood rushing through the chambers of her heart. Fluids gurgled through her throat during a gradual slowing of breathlessness to the point where she reached audible composure.

As soon as she was physically able, Carole would instinctively search for someone or something to hold on to. Her outstretched arms always found me quickly as her eyesight, hearing, and orientation began to return. Despite her desperate gasps for air at the start of recovery, she would always state breathlessly the words 'I'm OK, I'm OK, I'm OK' to let me know that she was exiting the seizure. She was always more concerned about letting us know that she was OK than for her own selfish need for air.

When I heard the OK, I would approach her outstretched arms and encircle her loosely with my own until her legs were strong enough for support of self. She always nestled her heavy head into my left shoulder, where she would happily stay for the next five minutes while the Carole we knew and loved returned to us – a little worse for wear but a little stronger for the experience.

After confirming that she was OK, but still in gasp, Carole would always ask about the children. She'd say, 'Where are they?' She'd ask me if they saw her seizure, and she'd want to know if they were OK. She'd ask me to let her know if that was 'a bad one or not', and then she'd apologise for putting me through another seizure. I used to cry, not because I shared her seizures in some sense or I could see what she couldn't, but because she was always beautifully unselfish. And then she'd cry because I was crying, and then I cried some more because I'd made her cry. We cried a lot that year, every teardrop devoted unconditionally to love.

It is difficult, maybe impossible, to contextualise the true psychological and physiological effects of seizure on Carole. She couldn't remember any of her sensory or emotional actions and reactions. This meant that she couldn't really interpret or translate how she felt through language or the use of comparative example.

As I observed the complexity of her experience, I could only imagine that it must've been like running a marathon in the midday heat of a dry desert without water before swimming across an ice-cold lake and then climbing to the top of the highest mountain without oxygen. Imagine doing all this in less than five minutes and having the instant fatigue associated with hours of very intense physical exertion. Then imagine doing this three or four times a day, sometimes for many days in succession. Then imagine yourself smiling through every recovery process so as not to intensify the pain on the faces of your loved ones. Imagine how much love it takes to do that – not once, not twice, but every time.

You will read a few times in this book that 'Just when you think you can't love anyone any more, they take the love you share up a few notches to another realm.' With every seizure, this is what I experienced. Carole was showing me that love knows no boundary. This was a tough but beautiful lesson that would rescue me again and again and again in the face of my own inferiority and adversity.

The first time we saw Carole seizure, it was almost impossible to reconcile imagery with reality, and yet the images were very real. The children and I hadn't known anything about epilepsy at the time, and innocently we'd had no need to know. On my first contact with the everyday form of epilepsy, I found myself in the same weird place I'd visited once before. It was when I was in hospital with Carole trying to explain the horrors of my visual theatre to her because she had no memory. Carole's internal defences wouldn't let her remember her seizures, and this was now a huge relief to me.

When I say she couldn't remember, she had a notion of horribleness and would describe her loss of vision as seeing white light and her loss of hearing as like listening to many thousands of voices all at the same time – each one undistinguishable from the others and all muffled together. She would remember exiting the seizure when recovery started and could describe the discombobulated sensation of becoming moderately human again. She would say that with each seizure, she felt less human and more uncomfortable with her general health. Maybe this discomfort was caused by her increasing awareness of the emotions of others through each interaction with her scream.

When I described what we saw externally, she was horrified. She wasn't concerned about herself – she never was. Carole was only ever concerned that her children were witnessing her horror and how this would affect them. Reluctantly, we agreed that it wasn't possible to shield them all the time, and as we'd promised not to hide things from them, we sought to manage as best we could the children's exposure to her illness.

We had two more loose ends that needed to be tied together – Carole's internal experience and our external view. We managed to tie this knowledge with ribbon and a bow, and it became another present we shared as a family to gain improved understanding day by day. The ribbon was Carole's containment of her own silent screams and the internalisation of the fear she felt for her children. The bow was her determined resolve to live her life fully and for us to live it with her. My job was to safeguard this present for all of us in a single timeless moment of life and love.

She used to emphasize the point with the children that even though they may see her have a seizure, she was, at the end of the day, still plain old Mummy. She was the same Mummy they'd always known and always loved and the Mummy who would still want to know why their bedrooms were untidy and if they'd done their homework. She was the same Mummy who had refused a new iPod because she might not like any of the songs on it. She was just Mum, and we loved her exactly the way she was.

Carole insisted that day-to-day life remain as normal as normal could be, whatever that would mean. Returning to the continuity of life before illness was the key to maintaining balance going forward, as was adapting to what going forward actually meant. We considered all the changes that we knew about, looked a little way into the future, and quietly made adjustments here and there. We taught the children basic first aid and how to put someone in the recovery position. Mobile phones were programmed with emergency numbers. We bought Carole a medical bracelet and a dog tag, and both were engraved with basic information that could be used in an emergency to save her life. I stayed at home for six weeks to oversee transitions while keeping a protective eye on my family. We were all getting to know our new house guest.

The children returned to school after the summer break. We followed the usual routine we'd adopted every year of leaving it until the last minute to buy all the new things they would need for the new term. Continuity was already at work! We all went shopping for shoes, uniforms, and stationery, at which point we realised that there was something else we needed to get used to. Epilepsy didn't have a conscience, and it couldn't tell the time.

Carole started to have seizures in public places. It was just one of those things that was unavoidable and part of getting used to change. Carole didn't care what people thought about her and adopted a healthy attitude to this, although she was naturally concerned for the rest of us. Complex partials were difficult for us to watch, but we had knowledge to help us manage through these events. To members of the public – and Carole's friends, who didn't necessarily have this insight – it was a little unsettling to witness Carole's distress during a seizure. If you've ever seen someone suffer a complex partial seizure, their behavioural characteristics may have appeared similar to those of someone intoxicated by recreational drugs or alcohol. Some people would just stare, some would offer help, and others wouldn't know what to do. None of this really mattered to us, as we knew why Carole was distressed and we knew what to do.

In crowded places sometimes, like shops and theme parks, Carole would need to find her light source, and she'd instinctively wander off in her state of scream. This made things a little awkward and uncomfortable for other people, as it often looked like our attempts to guide Carole to safety were doing the opposite. If Carole was ever comforted mid-seizure, her natural instinct was to push away, quite forcefully, the people trying to help her. Quite naturally, this was interpreted in the wrong way by passers-by. I guess people were reacting to sight but not to knowledge.

We used to say to people, 'It's OK, this is Carole, and she has epilepsy,' until we realised that people didn't actually know what epilepsy was! This was OK too, because if you think about it, why should they know?

One day, Carole walked to the shops as she always did to get bread and milk. Walking became part of her new morning routine, and she'd venture out in all weather. Everyone knew Carole by sight, and because of her love of talking and cheery disposition, she'd often chat to people she didn't necessarily know. If she'd bump into an old school friend, they'd usually have a natter for a few minutes and sometimes much, much longer!

On this particular occasion, she needed to visit the cash machine, and just as she'd inserted her cash card, she went into complex seizure. There were a few people in the queue behind her who must've wondered what on earth she was doing as she wandered off. Carole remembered holding her cash card and the stages of recovery but nothing else. She found herself surrounded by the lovely people who'd rescued her – one such lovely person relayed the information back to me years later.

On another day, she recalled herself exiting a seizure clinging to a lamp post on a busy main road not far from where we lived, only this time no one came to her rescue. She had no recollection of how she got to the lamp post but remembered a passer-by staring at her as she exited recovery. I dread to think what might have been. The public seizures made us rethink a few things, and we soon realised that Carole shouldn't really be left alone until we had a better handle on seizure control. I gave up my job in July 2010 to work with Carole as life took on a much deeper meaning day by day.

Carole was adjusting and coming to terms with all manner of things. Despite the difficulties and the adversity, she carried her humanity with her at all times. She never lost it or switched it off, although no one would've blamed her if she had. There were so many times when she could've just thrown in the towel, hidden away, given up, and lashed out at her nearest and dearest. Carole never did this.

One of the most difficult thing she eventually came to terms with was a gradual loss of her own independence. This drove her up the wall – not because her life was changing but because everyone else changed theirs in some way for her. She didn't like fuss, and she didn't want people fussing over her. Carole was always grateful for all the fuss, however, so much so that privately she would often cry about this. These were always happy tears, and she'd say, 'I have amazing people in my life. I don't deserve them.' I would tell Carole that it was her strength and love that inspired all of us to be there with her.

At other times, I'd catch her talking to herself. She'd say, 'So, I've got a brain tumour. I've got epilepsy. Now I can't bloody drive! Give me a break, guys, come on!' Then she'd smile and throw her hands in the air. 'It is what it is! I know, I know – it could be worse, much worse! Bloody brain tumour!' She was bloody amazing.

So we learned that epilepsy is mischievous, it has no conscience, can't tell the time, and has no regard for safety. We also learned that it rarely revealed the catalysts responsible for its sudden appearance and reappearance. We thought, however, that there might be some contributing factors to the onset of seizure. Temperature may have been one of them, as Carole started to have seizures at bath time. Loud noises were another. Playing computer games, diet, particular types of drinks, anxiety, stress, adrenaline-charged activities, and physical exercise were a few of the other considerations. There may have been any number of varying combinations of these things, or none of the above, which set seizures in motion. Most of these were manageable, to degrees, but each in its own right may have contributed a little more to her gradual loss of the independence she so desperately craved.

Independence was one of the things that had always defined her. Simple stuff that most of us take for granted started to be impacted. Carole was making dinner one evening – routinely chopping vegetables in the kitchen, as she'd done many thousands of time before – when complex partial stopped by. The children and I were in the lounge and Carole was on her own holding a large cook's knife. It wasn't until reaching recovery that she'd realised the potential seriousness of what might have been.

I would routinely call out to Carole if we were in separate rooms to make sure that she was OK. On this occasion, I got no reply and knew that something was wrong. Due to the rapid onset of the seizure and the immediate incoherence this caused, Carole never had an opportunity to call for help. I found Carole in breathless recovery. The knife was still in her outstretched hand.

'What if the children had tried to help me and I hurt them? I would never forgive myself,' she said afterwards. Carole was so distraught and totally beside herself with the 'what might have been' scenario that she never picked up a sharp knife again. To her absolute credit, she found alternative solutions for many things, even perfecting the art of making sandwiches using scissors.

* * *

The one part of Carole's life that she point-blankly refused to give up without a fight was her job. This was one of the many important things that were non-negotiable in Carole's world. Part of adjusting to meet the needs and constraints of illness was to look objectively and subjectively at the opportunity for her to carry on working. She'd always talk from the heart where the schoolchildren were concerned and would never compromise their safety to satisfy her own need to work.

I eventually understood her determination when one day she remarked, 'I've accepted so much, but the one thing I don't want anyone to take away from me is my job. It helps me to look forward.'

Against unfavourable odds, Carole was cleared by her senior medical team and the school authorities to continue to work at one of the local primary schools for an hour a day. School was about half a mile away from the house as the crow flies. Carole would walk there and back on most days to reconnect herself with nature and enjoy some private time alone with just her thoughts, birdsong, fresh air, and sunshine.

The trek to work took her through a small housing estate and down an unmade country lane where she'd bump into dog-walkers and other folk out for a midday stroll. I'd hear about all the interesting people she'd bumped into when she got home. More often than not, I would walk to school to meet Carole when she finished, and we'd walk back home together, hand in hand and rosy of cheek.

On days when the weather was unkind, I'd drop Carole off at work in the car or she'd cycle there under her own steam. Because physical fatigue was one of the possible catalysts for seizures, we had to be mindful of the dangers to Carole, and others, when she got on her bike. Occasionally she'd fall off her bike if epilepsy popped in unannounced, and one day she arrived at school covered in mud but otherwise OK. She used to tell me that she'd crawl to work on her hands and knees if she had to, and there were the odd handful of days when it must've looked like that was what she'd actually done. Somehow, Carole always managed to pick herself up, dust herself down, and smile. It was as though Carole had turned adversity into inspiration and never grew tired of proving to us and herself that life was for living – no matter what.

She loved her work, and she loved the children she worked with. As part of a small team, her role was to look after the children at lunchtimes and supervise the organisation of lots of fun activities in the playground. Carole knew all the children by name and cared for them in the same way as for her own children.

Although she worked for an hour a day for four days a week, her job started taking its toll on her physically. I don't think this was because the job was physically demanding. It probably had more to do with the fatigue caused by the build-up programme of drug therapy. As the weekly intake of drugs increased to optimise temporary protection from seizures, so Carole became more tired more quickly. She made a point of resting most afternoons to store up the energy needed for the following day.

We'd sit together and eat lunch on the sofa when she got home from work. It was at this time that I'd encourage Carole to tell me about the things she'd been doing and the people she met on her bumpy road. I did this so I had my own barometer for checking and balancing her memory and her general well-being. Sometimes she was so tired after work that she'd fall asleep mid-sandwich. We'd often talk about the practicalities of her continued employment from a safety perspective – not necessarily Carole's, more a case of the safety of the children in her care and the integrity of the school. Carole promised me that if she ever felt that these things were compromised, she would stop working.

As we progressed through illness, school was a lifeline for Carole in many ways. It gave her a sense of purpose, of self-worth, and of achievement. It was something that she looked forward to, and it was one of the very few constants of her life outside the security of our home and family. Above all else, it was a place that she enjoyed being. She loved school because as long as she didn't seizure in the presence of the children, she was always in the company of a little community of friends who simply knew her as Mrs Jones. Unbeknown to Mrs Jones, her little community of friends and colleagues would reciprocate her love for them one day in the most beautifully moving way.

In the other world where she lived, the one where she was known as Carole and as Mummy, there were always practical things to deal with and problems to solve. There were many metaphorical journeys where the potential existed to fall off her bike. Even though she always picked herself up, dusted down, and got back in the saddle, there were cuts and bruises and inevitably a few scars. One of these mental scars was etched by the nervous anticipation of a journey to hospital in London every few months for a magnetic resonance imaging (MRI) scan. The purpose of this appointment was simple: it was to check for signs of change to the size, shape, bulk, depth, and expansion of her glioma and to evaluate Carole's general well-being in the context of any change.

On the surface of things, this appeared to be a simple undertaking – but like Carole's dispersed glioma, the effects of scanning appointments were deeply invasive. They invaded the emotional, rational, intellectual, thinking, and seeing parts of Carole's life. They stripped back everything to expose Carole's deepest vulnerability. It filled her with a level of unparalleled, heartfelt fear every time. These appointments tested Carole's courage, mental strength, and resolve beyond limits that I never knew were possible. Gradually, Carole surrendered to her fear and released herself from it, but it did take a few appointments to achieve this.

Surrendering to fear is not a natural process for anyone, and she worked very hard with her inner child to do this. She'd always accepted her situation for what is was, but the opportunity always existed to discover that illness had entered a different path on her cycle through life. Carole and I knew that, in all reality, it would be at one of these appointments that we'd find out how bumpy our road really was. During times of invitational correspondence, our bicycle-made-for-two found itself on a one-way street heading for a place where stress lived. Even though we shared a healthy attitude towards managing stress levels in life, the certainty of living on a diminishing timeline increased the probability of getting some not-so-good news.

To Carole, these were scary moments. To me, they were really scary. My mirrored stranger was the only companion I could upset but not damage and I could throw bricks at without wounding. One day, he would help me find the answers to a million questions. In the meantime, I tried as best I could to be one of Carole's mirrors, to help find the answers to the difficult questions which she knew had to be asked. The letters from the hospital always prompted many questions.

Perhaps the two most important questions in times of correspondence were 'Everything will be OK, won't it, Bun? And what happens if it isn't?'

* * *

We had just about survived the first year living through a rapidly changing and dynamic life. We'd taken life one day at a time and managed our way through many new scenarios and a sea of storms and emotions. When we looked back over twelve months, Carole and I realised just how much change we'd been through as a family. It had taken a titanic effort from everyone.

We'd attended maybe three or four MRI scans in this period, and although some change to the glioma had been evidenced, the neurosurgical team were quietly observant about its slow progress. We would also attend other hospital appointments locally from time to time, usually between scans, to follow-up on cognitive health and Carole's general well-being. These appointments also carried nervous excitement, and it could be said that Carole found them stressful.

It occurred to me, driving home after a visit to the specialist epilepsy nurse, that we only ever discussed Carole's health in speculative terms at our medical meetings during those first twelve months. By this, I mean that we could only ever speculate about the number of seizures and their relative frequency because we hadn't kept any records. The MRI scan was the only factual image upon which tangible data could be analysed and made sense of – either as a snapshot in time, comparable from scan to scan, or by looking at the compound change from the very first scan through a series of milestones.

This gave us a scientific picture of health, which was great, but I wanted to know what this meant in real terms. I wanted to answer the questions that Carole felt were the most important ones, and I wanted to give her informed answers. Rightly or wrongly, I wanted to understand the relationship between drug therapy, seizures, and the scientific scan.

We'd been told not to associate the tumour with epilepsy for treatment purposes, but this never really sat well with me for logical and practical purposes. If Carole's seizure rates increased, it could be argued that there were changes in the glioma which could be proved, or disproved, by a scan. This might also suggest that Carole had become tolerant of the type and dosage of drugs, which could signal that an increased dosage was needed or a change to a new drug should be considered. If I could identify time-of-day seizure patterns or cross-reference seizure occurrence with events or activities in Carole's life, then maybe we'd be able to develop and manage a more cohesive approach to triggers and sustainable care.

I really wanted to know what worked, what wasn't working, and most of all to have some idea why. I decided it was important to have a better understanding of the real-life experiences of illness, and to get this I had to have data. I sat down with Carole, and we figured out between us what we needed to do.

Initially, Carole wasn't keen on the idea, saying, 'I live this stuff every day in my head, while I sleep, at work – everywhere! Why would I want to talk about it all the time?' I hadn't anticipated this response and knew immediately that Carole was perhaps being overcautious because she'd recognised that this type of data would also highlight negative change. I left the whole idea of data alone and prepared to let it go. Carole had enough to cope with, and in the overall scheme of things, it was Carole's choices that were important.

A week or so went by and then, out of the blue, she just said, 'Let's start recording things – you're right. We need to know if I'm getting worse.' This was a lovely example of our universal energies working in concert. She'd resisted and I went with her until she pushed and then I pulled.

Very quickly, I translated our requirements onto paper, and we started to collect information. We recorded and categorised daily seizure activity, the times of seizures, day vs night occurrence, and medication (the time it was taken and the dosage). After a while, we also noted any other information that might be significant – things like headache and birth-control medication, trips to the dentist, intense exercise, dietary change, walking or cycling to work, and anything that Carole considered to be different or unusual. We started to look at Carole's weight and BMI as general health indicators. The dates of medical appointments were also noted to see if she experienced more or fewer seizures during the periods just before, during, and after these meetings.

Soon, we had real data to look at on many different levels. We could see seizure patterns in terms of type and times. We could see the tangible effects of changes to drug dosage, and we could make recommendations to the medical staff about adapting, reacting to, or changing Carole's drug regime. We put BMI and weight graphs together and were able to overlay data to look at specific issues. All Carole had to do was remember to write down the time and type of seizure, and I did the rest. This might sound simple, but Carole was progressively losing her short-term memory. I had started to collect the information we needed to back up specific details for review purposes.

We began to develop a much more measured approach to the management and control of seizures. There were times when our analytical conclusions shaped changes to drug therapy and time-of-day dosage, which actually prevented seizures and broke up the pattern of repeated seizure activity. We even observed that Carole's birth-control medication was helping with seizure prevention. These were findings that contradicted the advice of one of the neurologists.

When we attended scanning appointments and the interim well-being appointments, we were able to talk with tangible authority about Carole's health. The medical teams monitoring Carole's epilepsy gave us licence to self-regulate changes to Carole's medication, which we were able to do insightfully as we had real data to work with. We were asked to work within certain time and dosage tolerances for safety purposes as long as we reported back our progress on a regular basis. This was so successful that at one point, Carole didn't experience any complex partial seizures for a period of eighty-four days consecutively. At other times, we achieved zero nocturnal seizures for a period of fifty-six days straight and zero simple partial seizures for a period of fifty days.

Aside from the analytical tools that we were evolving to help understand seizure patterns and drug usage, Carole was also learning physical techniques to suppress her seizures. Some of these techniques were brutal, but Carole was determined to try anything. Her resolve was always, 'If I can prevent just one seizure every now and again, it will prolong my life.'

In layman's terms, the underlying cause of epilepsy is believed to be abnormal electrical impulses in the brain, which malfunction in the form of electrical storms. These storms were what Carole referred to as feeling ticklish. The physical techniques of suppression are thought to divert the brain's attention away from the onset of storm. These techniques were brutal because it meant that Carole chose to inflict intense pain upon a part of her body to achieve suppression.

There were several pain points that she experimented with on her face, hands, and arms. She achieved mixed degrees of success but found it was frequently possible to suppress seizures. I would find her with lots of small scars on her arm where she'd dug her nails so deep into her skin that she bled. My heart bled to know that Carole would do this repeatedly of her own free will so that we didn't have to see her seizure.

I am not sure that I ever fully supported her 'no pain no gain' approach to seizure control, as the stress associated with intense physical pain may also have been one of the catalysts for seizure. It goes without saying, hopefully, that any changes to epilepsy treatments must always be discussed with trained medical professionals. Carole and I always sought both advice and permission to make changes, and we developed a solid relationship with the Carole's medical teams to define safe boundaries and tolerances within which to work.

The intervening weeks leading up to the day of Carole's scans were, for both of us, always a little wobbly. I guess this was to be expected. I knew when she was overthinking things, which was most days after she got her hospital letter, due to the regularity and depth of her questions. We'd talk constantly about the uncertainty ahead of us. As you might expect, Carole did most of the talking. I simply loved the fact that we could talk honestly and openly about anything and everything. We'd keep a lid on the date of the MRI scans and share this info with few people, just in case the outcomes were not so nice.

It would take us about an hour and a half to get to the hospital in London. It was always a journey that we had to make, and it was one of those changes to our life that was necessary. In the car, we'd recap what lay ahead, and I'd try to give Carole a measured response to her difficult questions: 'What happens if it's bad news? What if the drugs are controlling the seizures but masking the tumour? What if I need chemo? It will be OK, won't it, Bun?'

What I tried to do was just take Carole on a journey through her own mind. I'd prepare summaries for the meetings in London and memorise the data so I could replay the details back to Carole as we drove. She'd have all the data sheets in her hand so, based on believing is seeing, she could believe the details for herself. I'd be able to refocus her on the real facts: that over the last few months her seizure rate had declined day by day, or that even though seizure rates were the same she was experiencing more simple than complex. Sometimes changes to night-time meds had worked positively to reduce nocturnal seizures.

I'd be able to contextualise various things for her, and for the neurosurgical team, based on cold hard facts. This helped a little to take the edge off understandable concerns, which in turn helped her to relax. Carole would want to have the same conversation over and over again, but this was somewhat unavoidable, as remembering our earlier dialogue was a challenge for her. It was never an issue, because all Carole ever needed was to be heard, reassured and understood.

We'd usually arrive early for a scan and grab some lunch and a coffee in the hospital café. This little routine, usually fuelled by brie-bacon-and-tomato paninis, helped Carole adjust to her surroundings for the next few hours. Carole loved the whole process of scanning and was known to fall asleep mid-scan due to the gentle hypnotic oscillations of the imaging machine. Post-scan, Carole would be in a very relaxed state, which set her up nicely for the rest of the afternoon. She'd often emerge from the scan with Band-Aids dotted about her arms where her veins had collapsed. This was caused by multiple attempts to inject a suitable vein with the contrast medium used to make parts of her brain fluoresce.

Holding hands, we'd make our way down the long hospital corridor on the second floor to the stairs. Carole had a fear of travelling in lifts, so the stairs were always the safest stress-free option. On the ground floor, we checked in at the front desk of the glioma clinic and found some comfortable high-backed chairs, where we'd set up camp for the afternoon. We waited patiently for a few hours each time as per the progress of schedules and patient priority. We often recapped the conversations we'd had in the car and talk about life stuff, the normal stuff: what we were cooking later for our evening meal, what was going on at work and school, and how the kids were doing.

Carole was often sleepy during the afternoon anyway, and together with the aftereffects of therapeutic oscillation, being full from lunch, and being mellow on her afternoon cocktail of drugs, she needed a nap sometimes. A nap put her nervous anticipation to sleep too. She'd curl up next to me and rest her head on my shoulder as we surrendered unconditionally to whatever lay ahead.

We couldn't help but notice the other anxious faces around us. Perhaps we were all contemplating the same things. There were couples, mature ladies and gentlemen, and people on their own. There were parents with a child, a son or daughter; adult children with a parent or grandparent; and people there for their friends. We waited together. Perhaps we were all there at that time for a reason – as if time, space, and everything in between had bonded us for a few moments, minutes, and hours of shared heartache. Some emerged from their consultations with smiles, others with tears.

It was always a very quiet and peaceful place. The two of us marvelled at the resolve and cheery disposition of the hospital staff that graced the departments we visited. It takes a special kind of human to do what these lovely people do – kind humans indeed.

Carole's neurosurgeon, Mr White, always collected his patients personally from the waiting room, and he'd look for each one as he rounded the small corner from his consulting room. Carole always knew when it was her turn. We had a sort of arrangement with regard to bags, coats, and other possessions; Carole would leave them all to me, so I'd follow her eager rush to the room always three paces behind. Mr White and Carole had got to know each other quite quickly during the first few appointments. Because she'd quite naturally exhibit some external signs of stress at the beginning of these meetings, I think Mr White realised that he needed to cut to the chase fairly quickly in terms of the scan and its bottom line. Intuitively, he did this very expertly before furnishing us with specifics.

After these meetings, which usually lasted between twenty to thirty minutes, Carole insisted that we pop back to the hospital café and buy two slices of cake to take home. She wanted the children to associate our trips to the hospital with something nice. Cake always has that magical ingredient that somehow makes everything better – just like a mother's love.

At the end of the ground-floor foyer was a discreet and quiet area where Carole would phone her Mum and share her news. It was at this spot that she'd also text friends to let them know that she was OK and that she had lived to fight another day. Her phone beeped regularly with messages of love and support during the journey home.

We were always relieved to send anxiety, stress, and fear on a short but deserved vacation until the next cycle of correspondence. Carole always cried on our way back to the children after the trips to London. At these times, the light that usually shone so brightly within Carole seized its opportunity to shine brighter than ever before. She released all of her emotions to fly freely without condition and encouraged her tears to wash heartache away.

I imagined Carole's tears as rainbow-coloured butterflies whose wings would carry her love on every summer breeze of destiny across the wild-flower meadow of my heart. To see her eyes sparkle at these moments was breath-taking and beautiful. They say the most beautiful eyes have cried the most tears. I'd have to say that the purest hearts have the most beautiful eyes, for they allow us to see, feel, and dream of life in its most vulnerable but beautiful form – to see love.

5

The Dream That Came True

Carole loved the theatre. She loved the atmosphere and the sense of occasion. It was her ultimate place of relaxation and enjoyment, a place where she felt she belonged. I'm not quite sure I can explain her connection to the theatre, but the connection was strong, almost magnetic. She liked to arrive early for each show and soak up the atmosphere as the seats filled up. The sound of lofty acoustics excited her, as did the dimming of house lights, the echo of universal silence, and the anticipation of first breath.

We'd arrived early at the theatre in Woking, and Carole and I found our A24 and A25 seats front left of the stage three rows back with a perfect view. The theatre filled up slowly as we sat browsing the *Svengali* programme together. Carole and I had been to see Derren's shows on three other occasions, and each had been a very special, enjoyably entertaining evening.

The last time we'd been to see him, an opportunity to take part in the show literally fell in my lap. I had dodged one of Derren's Frisbees as he threw a sidewinder to the upper tier in the theatre at Reading. As it arced its way towards me, the people seated behind us all reached over my head to grab it – and then it fell awkwardly into my lap. I'm quite a shy chap; to anyone else, this might have been a wonderful moment, but at the time it was a little unnerving for me to say the least. The most entertaining dinner guest in history or possibly the scariest man on Earth was about to talk to me.

Notwithstanding a few nervous moments, I found myself involved in the show at ad hoc intervals throughout the evening without having to leave the comfort of my seat or the protective hand of my lovely and very excited wife. The whole experience that evening was actually amazing in the end – not only for me, but for Carole as well.

As we sat in our seats in Woking, reminiscing about the Frisbee-catching abilities of the people behind us, we were approached by one of Derren's team. He chatted about a particular part of the show and asked us if we wanted to write down on a piece of paper one of our most embarrassing moments. All we had to do was jot it on the back of a piece of paper, fold it in half, and pop it into the bucket he was holding.

Carole, of course, grabbed the pencil and paper and promptly began writing something down – something about strawberry yoghurt, I think! I quietly declined, and the guy said he'd pop back later to collect Carole's piece of paper. In the meantime, Carole finished writing and convinced me I should take part.

'It's just a bit of fun!' she said. 'Besides, no Frisbees in sight, and lightening doesn't strike the same place twice!' But we weren't in the same place! She gave me one of her 'for me' looks and smiled with her eyes … those gorgeous eyes of contagious optimism got me every time. How could I refuse?! When the guy came back just a few minutes later, I borrowed Carole's pencil, wrote something down, and sheepishly handed in my paper.

I turned to Carole and said, 'There you go, just for you. Happy Christmas!' Then I said jokingly, as if to tempt fate and a second bolt of lightning, 'If they read out my note, you know it will probably ruin my evening.' She laughed with me – or was that at me? Not sure! Without a second thought, we picked up the programme and had just a few minutes left to browse again before the houselights dimmed. Carole squeezed my hand during the echo of silence before the music started and the show burst into life.

We sat there together having a magical time. After about ten minutes, a member of the audience seated in the front row was chosen at random to select one of the pieces of paper from the bucket of embarrassing moments. One was promptly selected and placed into an envelope that was then sealed. The show continued. Derren wandered offstage during various segments of the show to connect personally with his audience. When he did this he stood right in front of Carole and was literally centimetres away from her on three or four occasions.

As he stood there, she kept looking at me, pointing very discreetly with the index finger on her right hand, and mouthing the words, 'That's Derren Brown! That's Derren Brown!' When he returned to the stage after Carole's first encounter with him, she whispered in my ear, 'Now my evening is complete!'

We were having a great time, and Carole was in a lovely place. I was relaxed but ever more conscious of her excitement. She'd successfully managed to suppress a few seizures throughout the day, which either meant that she was OK for the rest of the evening or that it was only a matter of time before a nasty one showed up. I would've liked her to rein in some of that excitement and be a little more grounded, though I didn't say anything because she was having such a fab time. To see her carefree and wonderfully happy in one of her favourite places and in the company of a great man – and Derren! – was a magical gift in itself.

The 'most embarrassing moment' part of the show was upon us. The same audience member from the front row was handed back the envelope and asked to read the slip of paper out loud. Derren had us all stand up and instructed us not to react if the information we were about to hear was in fact our own. The audience was on its feet, and we all listened anxiously as the house lights were lowered to virtual darkness. Derren stood onstage now with a powerful flashlight that he shone across his house guests for the evening.

As I stood there with Carole to my right, she elbowed me very gently and whispered, 'Don't worry – it won't be you. Relax!'

I was thinking, *Here we go, any second now it's gonna be ...* and then it happened.

I wasn't sure what to do. Had my ears deceived me? The guy was reading from my piece of paper! I'm guessing there must have been at least 1,100 people in the theatre, maybe more. The guy read it again, and then Derren repeated what he had said. Lightning struck me twice! And they say there's no such thing as a coincidence. Ha!

Carole tapped my right hand with the little finger on her left. Apart from this, neither of us dared move, but I could sense her rolling about in the aisles of her own mind laughing her head off. Quietly and in total disbelief, I waited.

I had that awful feeling you get when you're about to get your school exam results and you hope that you get someone else's by mistake. Somehow, in between the printing of the results slip and it being delivered to you, you just hope that the grades magically change as you open the envelope.

After selective questioning of the main body of the audience, there were only three people left standing. My face had been projected onto a large screen, and the flashlight dancing in my eyes was blinding – and just a little intimidating. Carole, by this time, was seated, and out of the corner of my eye I could see her staring at me with the cheekiest of cheeky grins. I'd managed to lower my heart rate just enough to speak with audible composure, and for a moment attention was placed on the other two guys still standing. I realised very quickly that I was just being lulled into a false sense of security by a man who was, without any doubt, the master of his craft. The three of us were still standing when a very special and unexpected thing happened. Derren stopped and smiled, pointing the flashlight at Carole.

'Ah! The lady sitting next to you!' he said, pointing at me. 'Please stand up!' He was laughing. 'Maybe I was wrong,' he said. 'Maybe it was a lady after all.' She'd caught his attention because she'd found it almost impossible to contain her excitement. The cheekiest of cheeky grins was now even cheekier!

As this particular feature of the show neared its conclusion, Derren spoke faster and more excitedly, but he changed to a softer tone when he spoke to Carole. Her face was now on the big screen as a few gentle questions floated in her direction – some subtle misdirection and some honest dishonesty, methinks! The other two guys were asked to sit down. I think that was the point I knew I was in trouble. Derren knew that I knew it was only a matter of time. Then both our faces were onscreen, and the flashlight shone back and forth from Carole to me. Finally, he let a very giggly Carole sit down. As she sat, she circled her left arm around the inside of my right thigh, where it stayed sympathetically for the remainder of the time I was on my feet.

Before I did anything else, I looked at Carole and mouthed the words, 'You OK?'

She replied, 'Yep, sorry Bun!'

Derren being Derren, not content with showing off his exquisite skill in the art of deduction, decided that he'd take my embarrassing moment to a higher level of entertainment by deducting the mathematical significance of my handwritten note – very impressive indeed! An act of absolute brilliance! After another embarrassing moment, I returned to the comfort of my seat. The first half of the show was over. It was time for ice-cream, although a very large Scotch would have also been in order!

We grabbed some refreshments and a bottle of water so that Carole could take her epilepsy medication discreetly during the intermission. Over ice-cream, we replayed the first half of the show. Carole was still on cloud nine or maybe somewhere at the very height of our little universe. She would remain on her adrenaline-, ice-cream-, and now drug-induced high for a little while longer. We sat back in our seats, held hands, and thoroughly enjoyed the rest of the show. It was truly wonderful – and the show was amazing too!!

As we made our way out of the auditorium into the crispness of night under a clear sky, Carole turned to me and said, 'There's just one more thing I'd like to do. I might never have this opportunity again – follow me.'

As we talked to figure out which way we needed to go, our breath smoked dragon-like from mouth and nostrils. It was teeth-chatteringly cold. The stage door was only a short walk around the corner, and when we arrived we found ourselves third or fourth in line. Within a few more minutes, an orderly queue had formed behind us. Our fellow autograph-hunters were all friendly and each equally excited at the prospect of meeting Derren in person. There was a lovely buzz in the air as people exchanged details on how many times they'd been to see the show, which show was their favourite, and how it was mesmerising to see Derren do the things he does with such mystery and mastery. One lady in particular was more excited than most – the one holding my hand!

Whenever we went out together, I couldn't help but be on high alert just in case gentle assistance was needed. This never got in the way of fun or enjoyment and had become just one of those things, an extra thought process or two here and there. Given the magical surroundings in which Carole found herself that evening – the sudden change in temperature, the occasional adrenaline surge, her fatigue, and the small fact that within the next twenty minutes Carole would again be standing right next to Derren Brown – the probability for seizure was a little higher than average. But I needn't have worried. Carole was unperturbed, and nothing, not even a tickly brain, was going to get in the way of realising the second part of one of her greatest life ambitions. We hugged for most of the time while we waited as I attempted to keep her warm.

After a short time, Derren appeared and was engaging, receptive, and charming with his adoring fans. Carole kept squeezing my arm until it was her turn. She presented her programme for autograph, and Derren wrote, 'To Carole, lots of love, Derren X.'

As he scribbled away, Carole turned to him and with her own natural girly but sophisticated charm simply said, 'I hope this doesn't sound sycophantic, but I think you're fabulous!'

'Oh! Thank you very much,' was his immediate reply.

As he handed her back the programme, she seized upon this moment of perhaps once-in-a-lifetime opportunity and asked, 'Thank you! And – can I have a cheeky kiss?'

'Yes, of course,' he said, and with that Derren kissed Carole gently on her cheek and gave her a hug – a really wonderful moment and a treasured memory that Carole held deep in heart. What a lovely man!

They thanked each other again. I thanked Derren and shook his hand, and then Carole and I headed off in the direction of the car park. She was heady with excitement and a little higher on life than she had been just a few minutes earlier, when she was already as high as a kite. Beautiful! What was equally beautiful is that for the rest of the evening, Carole's invisible friend of seizure was a no-show.

When I look back upon our evening of wonders of 16 March 2011, I can't help but cry a few happy tears. Carole had achieved one of her greatest life ambitions. Her memory of that day, the show, her involvement in it, speaking to and meeting with one of her real-life heroes if not the greatest influence on her late life, her signed programme, her cheeky kiss and hug – all these things remarkably never left her memory. Perhaps a little magic of her own was conjured to do this. For the rest of Carole's life, she would feed off the experience of meeting Derren, and it showed her she could do almost anything if she put her mind to it. My memory of that evening with Carole, to see her face, to hold her hand, and to feel the abundant energy of her excitement all around is also a very beautiful memory and one that will never leave me.

When I think about how all of the individual moments of that evening were somehow woven together, and how they were manifested before our very eyes, I can't help but think that there really is a little more to life than meets the eye. If we hadn't been in the company of the ultimate, the all-time favourite, and the most admired celebrity of Carole's world, I might think we'd been a little lucky that evening. Given the unique talents of the aforementioned gentlemen, I have to say that I'm a little baffled – in Carole-speak, I'm certainly kafuffled. Most importantly, I'm just so very, very grateful.

Perhaps, just perhaps, in the realm of our consciousness, an evening with Derren Brown is never just a coincidence – or is it?! I'll leave you with just one other thought for the time being. It's one that keeps me kafuffled. Perhaps there were other moments of illusion and mastery in the theatre that evening which were created magically for a very beautiful lady. Just a thought!

6

Beautiful You

Throughout Carole's illness, we were able to talk openly and pragmatically about every aspect of our life that had been impacted by a future that was certain but filled with uncertainty. Although this was painful and often unsettling, there was a lovely connection between the two of us that found reassurance, understanding, and above all else a unique bond that melted our hearts together. The one thing Carole would never talk about was what we would need to do on our day of reckoning. What I would do. What she would want me to do.

Our evenings together were always simple and filled with a richness that, now when I think about them, is difficult to describe in words but is so wonderful to feel emotionally. Without warning, I find myself drifting back through a cranial brochure of the most vivid and colourful pictures, thoughts, and voices that fashion both a warm smile and a trickle of tears. I smile because of Carole's beautiful outlook in the face of her tick-tock finality and the way she transformed the most difficult conversations into facts of life rather than crisis. I cry out of sadness for the happy-go-lucky girl whose determination to live, love, and be loved was steadfastly her only ambition. I'm lucky to have the ability to remember. I am rich in memory, spoiled by experience and love.

Carole found a sort of sanctuary doing crosswords and other types of writing or interactive puzzles that challenged her mental capacity and memory skills. She set two simple objectives for these evening vocations: to proactively stimulate her processing and memory functionality, and to assess changes to her brain's general functioning and ability to cope with simple and repetitive tasks. Carole's philosophical outlook on the development or continuity of her brainpower was simple and straightforward. If she could maintain an ability to think laterally, to solve problems, and to complete intellectual tasks on a regular basis, she would be reassured of her health. That assurance would stimulate positive thought and stave off her obvious and quite natural paranoia about tumour growth. The other thing, of course, that crosswords and brain puzzles did was draw her thoughts temporarily away from the incessant turmoil of illness and mortality.

Playing the piano daily was another of Carole's self-styled barometers for proving to herself that the left and right sides of her brain were continuing to work in concert with each other. Given the location of tumour dispersed throughout the right frontal lobe, she was determined to find ways to identify the most acute changes to motor skills, coordination, memory, and also eyesight. Carole wanted me to believe that her early identification of changes would allow timely medical intervention that might prolong her life. She silently tuned her physical and emotional sensors to detect the micro-signals that might expose the advancement of her mortal enemy within.

I loved listening to Carole tinkle the ivories, and she used me, sometimes, as her tone-deaf tape recorder when she wasn't sure that all was well. Carole selected three of her most favourite piano scores and played them routinely without fear. She played Beethoven's 'Quasi una fantasia' – his piano sonata no. 14 in C sharp minor. Its title translates to 'Almost a Fantasy'. Carole was born to play this music, and when she played it was as if her soul danced in exaltation of something most fantastic. It is said that when Beethoven played this piece, he was reminded of the moonlight reflected off Lake Lucerne, Switzerland. As Carole seated herself on her white piano stool, the music conjured a nocturnal scene in my head of the gentle ripple of moonlight at lake's edge and the distant echo of ethereal voices.

Most people know 'Quasi una fantasia' today by its more popular title, 'Moonlight Sonata'. Beethoven dedicated it to Countess Giulietta Guicciardi, the lady of his dreams. Giulietta and Beethoven would escape each other's reality despite their deepest love for one another. Carole played this sonata with the heart of a woman in love with life – beautiful synchronicity, perhaps.

Carole also brought to life Scott Joplin's 'The Entertainer' and Johann Pachelbel's Canon in D major to complete her daily repertoire. Canon in D major was one of our all-time personal favourites – so much so that it was played at our wedding. Today, for me, this has so much value of memory and invokes warmth and love every time I hear it. Coincidental, maybe, that this particular piece was an important part of Carole's own history, as it featured at the beginning, throughout, and toward the end of a journey through her own moonlight fantastic. Both of us were lucky enough to understand, acknowledge, and appreciate the opportunity to live out our fantasy life together. I got to love my fairy tale princess in a place where reality and illusion were juxtaposed among midnight stars, underscored only by the vibration of love and the light of the moon.

Most days, without her knowledge, I would stop whatever I was doing, wherever I was doing it, and listen quietly to her piano poetry as the magical sound fluttered through the house. Each ascending note, crotchet, and quaver would resonate with every beat and resting pause of my heart. I would pop my head around the lounge door and observe Carole's reflection in the mirror that hung above the open brick fireplace and smile as she sensed my protective gaze. Carole continued to play with a short turn of head, a stern but facially funny and silent rebuke that let me know that she knew I was there and that I should be doing something less boring instead.

If I ignored her gentle suggestion to leave, she returned my smile, usually muttering humorously under her breath the words 'Go away, Bun!' I always did, of course, but usually after a cheeky grin or a thumbs-up sign – sometimes both. I'd realised quickly that interrupting Carole's piano time was never a wise thing to do, although this never stopped my heart's delight at the audible joy created by Carole's fingers as they skipped, hop-scotched, and danced fairy-like across her most treasured possession.

Carole's piano reminds me in so many ways of Carole. Her piano is a creation of timeless beauty. It is rare, upright, and finely tuned. It is simply black and white. Its exterior is plain, and yet every corner, every curve and straight edge forms a structure that is elegant, solid, reliable, and fit for a purpose. It never let her down. On the inside, it is an instrument of perfection, each moving part delicately tuned and balanced with precision by a master craftsman, with care and with so much love. Every moving part has a job, a place, a dependency, and interdependency.

Her piano was the core of Carole's universe, and just like the universe, when trusted and embraced unconditionally, it revealed its magic at the hand of someone deserving, humble, skilled, and sensitive, someone with a pure heart and a soul that longed to sing songs of love. The piano revealed Carole's soul as every note she commanded from her mechanical companion vibrated through her entire body, awakened all of her senses, and emitted music fit for the ears of angels.

Carole was my universe. She openly revealed its vibrations and secrets to me throughout our life together. She was my music and my song, lifelong. Carole's soul flies throughout my world every day with each memory of her piano time. My sense of memory and emotion are now awakened through the flutter of our children, who command Mummy's piano to play with the same magical and enchanted resonance. Their mastery invites my soul to sing and my heart to stream with every note of memory and presence.

* * *

One particular evening, the children were safely tucked in bed and fast asleep. I browsed the TV channels for something interesting to watch as Carole relaxed with a crossword book. She wore her dainty thin-rimmed rectangular glasses balanced expertly toward the end of her nose so that it was possible to look over the top of them, without handling them, when switching from reading to talking. When she did this she looked wise, like a teacher with wisdom beyond her years. We'd often sit together on the sofa and just hold hands in the comfort and silence of our togetherness as we undertook our individual activities. This particular evening was no exception.

Carole always sat in a sort of sideways kneeling position with her right foot tucked underneath her bottom, probably to keep it warm. If the tingly sensation of pins and needles ever affected her right foot, she'd simply swap to the opposite sideways posture and tuck in the left foot instead. Over the course of a crossword marathon, she swapped posture many times.

Carole was deep in concentration with gaze fixed on the pages in front of her, glasses balanced, pen in her right hand. The top of the black biro rested gently on her bottom lip in between a pattern of rhythmic pen taps that announced an occasional thought or mutter of inspiration. I decided that perhaps it was time to broach another potentially awkward conversation as I held her left hand with my right.

I squeezed her hand gently for a few seconds, prompting her to look up from her puzzle book.

She smiled at me and said, 'You OK, Bun?' We exchanged a fixed gaze momentarily, during which she instinctively knew that something was on my mind. 'What's up?' she said intuitively. 'I know that look!' Carole and I knew each other so well that at times it was like we were the same person. I paused and continued to look directly into the striking hazel eyes exposed above her glasses by her forward-tilted, inquiring brow. She squeezed my hand back saying, 'Talk to me, what's wrong?'

In reply, I said, 'I've been thinking about a few things, and I want to chat about something but I'm not sure what to say or even how to say it. It's been on my mind a lot.' She put down her black biro and held my right hand now with both her hands. 'You know I love you,' I said. 'And you know that sometimes we have to have difficult conversations about where we are with our life, and that these things are things that won't go away.'

Carole now put down her puzzle book on the floor and turned to face me. She resumed holding my right hand with both of hers, and she'd switched to a crossed-leg position, as had I. As we faced each other like two meditating Buddhas, I put my left hand on top of her hands and said, 'Carole, I need to know what to do.'

She looked puzzled, but there were no cross words, just 'I'm not sure what you mean.'

'On the day that my world collapses, I need to know what you want me to do.'

She replied so matter-of-factly, 'You mean on the day that I die.'

'Yes, on that day,' I said.

There was a short pause. She gripped my hands with what felt like a grip of fear and of love as her eyes glazed over. Carole's reply was not what I had expected; indeed, I hadn't really known what to expect, but I certainly didn't anticipate what she said next. In hindsight, I guess there may have been nothing else that she could have said.

'I don't want to talk about it, Bun. I don't think I ever will.' Carole's voice was soft and assured. She was absolute in her message and looked me straight in my eyes. Her next sentence was equally emphatic. 'As hard as it may be for you, Bun, you will know what to do. I'm sorry. I trust you.'

Carole gave me one of her lovely but awkward smiles. Her glistening eyes opened wider than they would normally as she pouted her bottom lip to the right and pinned it in place for a few seconds with her front teeth before searching the ceiling for inspiration. She sighed and whispered to the heavens, returning to look at me directly with a loving shrug of the shoulders. Facially, she sent me the message *please don't go there*. I knew not to question or try to develop the conversation any further.

As I looked beyond Carole's glasses and deep into her eyes, there was another moment that felt like her soul spoke to me. It was a moment of sadness and song, a moment of confusion and absolute clarity. A moment perhaps of greater understanding cemented by a statement that I will never forget: 'I will never say goodbye to you, Bun. I can't explain. In time, you will understand.'

Carole let go of my hands, transitioned from dropped lip to smile, and tapped me comically twice on the inside of my right thigh, saying, 'Fancy making us a coffee then?' She picked up her book and pen from the floor and assumed her sideways posture with right foot once again tucked away. She put the black biro back to her lips, and as I kissed her forehead, she just said, 'Love ya, Bun.'

As I departed the lounge for the kitchen, my legs turned to jelly and my stomach tied itself in knots. I glanced back at her reflection in the glass-panelled door leading from the lounge to the hallway and caught sight of a moment of shared heartache for both of us. Carole was wiping a tear from her right eye as it escaped beneath her glasses to the tune of a single sniff. She must have seen my observance reflected in the door, and she turned her head in my angled direction. She just said, 'How's that coffee getting on?'

'It's on its way,' I sniffled back.

Our conversation that evening put a few things into perspective for me. It let me know that there were boundaries even for the most courageous heart. It emphasised in a uniquely definitive way that Carole was fragile and brave, that she was sensitive and that she hurt. I felt guilty, so guilty, for bringing up the matter of her pending finality and was absorbed negatively in my own selfishness for the minutes I spent on my own in the kitchen.

I stared at the image of my stranger in the kitchen window. He stared back at me perplexed. We were torn between our overwhelming desire to understand and to take care of Carole's last wishes, to do the right thing for our best friend, and to make sure that simple details were in order. We were compelled by nothing other than the deepest love to seek help making some of the toughest decisions. We were desperate to do the right things to take care of a beautiful life, create a lovely legacy, and preserve, gift-wrap, and protect memories for the children.

In the kitchen, I realised that my selfishness and guilt were not entirely misplaced and that we'd needed to have this conversation. I needed to feel those emotions and, in a strange way that I couldn't explain at the time, I needed to listen to the voice in my heart and embrace the message she gave me. She was telling me, subliminally or otherwise, to be strong, to not worry unnecessarily, and to focus on taking care of my girl for the rest of our life together.

If Carole was OK then life was OK. Everything else was secondary. While on the surface I appeared to have received no help from Carole that evening, I actually received all the answers I would ever need. Carole had helped me more than I could ever have known in those moments because a stage had been set, a precedent observed, expectations levelled, and in a peculiar way, one of my many fears expelled.

Sometimes the chaos and adversity of life take over and are all-consuming, and I felt on that particular evening that I hadn't really stopped to think about the opposites of these things. Maybe I had – I didn't really know. All I can say is that my heart had done my thinking for me, and I surrendered to it unconditionally in a moment when I wanted some answers. Perhaps it was simply that Carole's heart had guided me to the answers she knew I needed. Perhaps she was showing me the method, the silent internal madness of her genius, a map, a route, or a strong principle that would reveal something about her, about life, or about both of us. I think we had found equilibrium for our inner conflict.

Sometimes things just happen in a particular way for no other reason than to show or teach. Sometimes nothing makes sense and yet everything has sensitivity. Trying to fathom this stuff can, at times, be a lesson in futility unless you can force a hefty degree of relaxation and unconditional surrender of your innermost fears.

Carole had put her trust in me to take care of things. As difficult and as emotionally challenging for me to accept as it was at the time, Carole had given me the most beautiful compliment I could ever ask for. She let me know very gently that she thought I was worthy of her, and so she nourished my heart's own unselfish all-seeing appetite with her love. My acceptance and understanding of this was all that Carole needed to feel. I gave Carole this reassurance a few minutes later. I also gave her coffee.

We sat on the sofa for the remainder of the evening in communion, holding hands. All I could think about was love and how much I loved and was loved. Occasionally, Carole would tilt her furrowed brow forward, peer over the top of her glasses, and ask, 'You OK, Bun?' as I worked out another silent part of my never-ending jigsaw puzzle.

I replied, as always, 'I'm OK, I've got you. You OK?

Carole replied, 'I'm OK, we've got each other.'

That evening, Carole solved a beautiful mystery for me. In my world, Carole's love was the musical vibration of her life. The puzzle she helped me to complete was indeed beautiful. It had two beautiful halves of perfect symmetry. It was the unheard symphony that resonated with my heart, waiting patiently for Carole's fingertips to bring it to life. The symphony had always been there, and it grew stronger and louder with the presence of each day with her.

I realised that I understood more about love than ever before, and I understood this because Carole had taught me. To understand Carole, I had 'to get her', and 'together' we understood. We knew our hearts had always vibrated at the same compassionate and unconditional frequency for each other, reflecting with equal measure and with perfect pitch the beautiful music of life, the sound of love.

For One More Day

It was Monday, 14 November 2011. I was missing Carole so very much. Another busy day beckoned me with the noise of alarm. The Jones household swung into the routine it had been forced to adopt for the past week. I was the lone parent organising, coordinating, and just about managing the daily rigour of family life single-handedly and not enjoying a second of it without my best friend.

The day was a whirl of school uniforms, washing, cleaning, cooking for three instead of four, comforting, caring, talking, and reassuring my little ones that we were OK and that Mummy was OK because she was in the best possible place to get the medical care that was right for her. Even though it hurt that we were separated from Mummy, we had to be patient. I'd convinced myself that if the children were OK, I was OK, and Carole would be OK. That morning, as far as I could tell, we all were.

My constant anxiety over Carole's waning health, her general well-being, and her temporary separation from all of us weighed so heavily. It was in every thought process, in every activity, everything that we were now simply unable to share with her and her with us. Carole and I had only ever been parted for a few days and nights throughout our entire life together. To be separated now for a week, even though I saw her for a few priceless hours every day in hospital, was just so tough. I missed the simple things like Carole's smile in the morning, her wonderful facial expressions, her laugh, the lazy and unmistakable sound her slippers made paddling the wooden floor in the hall. I longed for Carole's conversation, her insight, her infectious humour, hugs, and cuddles; being outplayed on Wii golf; the tinkling of ivories; my goodnight kiss and my voice of assurance.

The children missed Carole in every way. They missed watching Mummy sleep on the sofa in the afternoons as her drugs kicked in, sending her to deep slumber and seizure-free recuperation for a few precious hours. They were unable to cover her up lovingly with their blankets as she slept peacefully in the lounge while they kept her company, doing their homework with the softest whisper and considerate movements so as not to wake her.

Carole always tried her hardest, most of the time successfully, to make sure that she was awake to greet the children when they arrived home at the end of their school day. This was what she lived for. She beamed from ear to ear with eyes wide and sparkling upon their return, eager to hear everything about their day. We all missed being there for her when perhaps she needed us the most. We missed her being there for us.

The daily ringing of all the alarms around the house that we'd set on phones, watches, and clocks in different places at different times to remind us to remind Carole to take her medication were now eerily silent. The seizure sheet we completed daily had no entries past Sunday 6 November. Even the shared experience of seizure was now absent, and despite the fact that they were terrifyingly horrible to watch, we'd all got used to them being part of our life. Together, we'd adapted to manage them as routinely as possible, and oddly, it was equally horrible without our house guests.

I would sometimes hear the children shout out 'Dad, Dad – Mum's having a seizure' or in extreme circumstances just the words 'Dad – now!' and then calmly do the things I always did to reassure the children and Carole that everything was going to be OK. Helping Carole recover from every complex partial seizure was so moving for all of us that it served, without a spoken word, to bond us even more tightly than we'd ever dreamed possible. Seizure had been our critical friend on most days and was just another one of our constant visual reminders of the fragility of life. Positively, they personified Carole's cast-iron determination to take each seizure in her stride one by one, day after day after day. As a family, we'd grown the abnormal into our normality, and since Carole had been in hospital, our world was no longer normal, even though it was very real.

Over the last week, our routine had changed, and we'd had no choice but to flex again to something I despised but had to embrace and accept. My new routine gave me a glimpse of what life would feel like, look like, and be like in our not too distant future. This glimpse was just about palatable on the basis that it was only short-term while Carole was being cared for by her team of dedicated professionals.

There was an odd and uncomfortable familiarity about not having Carole at home that had caused me deepest consternation over the previous weekend. This had been on my mind so much, and although there was now a sure-fire inevitability about our family's post-Christmas predicament, I didn't want to get used to the idea of being without my soulmate just yet. I never wanted to get used to this – not then, not ever – and my contemplation of this fact, even for just a few seconds, was soul-destroying.

I had been reluctantly conditioning myself during the last two years to face the darkest of days without Carole. All I could do was hope that I'd find her courage and the personal strength to adopt her 'just get on with it' attitude. When you live through adversity with the people you love, you become so tuned-in to the smallest of changes in character, health, behaviours, and communication that it's impossible not to recognise the positive and negative in all areas of family life. All change is good as long as it can be managed effectively most of the time. That's what I kept telling myself, anyway. In nature, if nothing ever changed, there would be no butterflies.

For me, the important thing was to be aware of change, understand the relative significance and root causes, and then try to rationalise quickly what this meant to each of us individually and to our family dynamic. Putting practical and workable solutions in place, however, for the different types of change was something else entirely. Managing change emotionally under circumstances which themselves changed too frequently in a short time frame had been tough.

In my heart, I knew that this would only get tougher because Carole was unable to help me recognise, negotiate, contextualise, share, and manage these changes. What I was beginning to understand, though, was that Carole's example of 'just deal with things and adapt' was the inspiration I was relying on now to get me through each day. Carole was in the right place for the moment, and even though we were heartbroken by our temporary separation, she trusted me to do the right things at the right time.

Without my knowledge, Carole had woven her love and belief in me through my core every day during her adversity, in fact throughout our life together, so that I had her emotional and mental toolkit. This toolkit emerged slowly as Carole's health deteriorated. It helped me to focus on and balance our immediate priorities, and it put life values in plain context. I was oblivious to all of this at the time, but now I recognise the depth of Carole's teaching. I was able to ride on my carousel of challenges for one more day every day because I had a great teacher. My teacher was Carole, and her teacher was love.

As I prepared breakfast for the three of us that morning, I flashed back to a wonderful memory of one of the loveliest things Carole had ever said to me. We were standing together in the kitchen one day preparing food just as I was doing then on our joint behalf. I caught Carole momentarily staring at me. Brilliant sunshine cascaded through the kitchen window, illuminating her freckled face. She stood adjacent to the kitchen sink, facing me. In my visual playback, she is radiant in a way that I'd never seen before – a perfect picture of health. This was both beautiful and unnerving at the time. She had a faraway look in her eyes, as if she was about to seizure. I remember stopping whatever it was I was doing and walking the few steps toward her open embrace, my eyes fixed on her smile. She flung her arms around my neck so tightly that her elbows met each other at the back of my head.

In the next moment, my dream girl squeezed me with the most sensual hug to whisper with pillowy softness the most beautiful words to escape her lips: 'You're not the best-looking man in world or the smartest man in the world, and you're not the fittest man in the world, but you are my man, and I know you will always be there for me. And you know I will always love you and that I always have.'

I held Carole in my arms and lost myself in her eyes. I remembered thinking I never wanted that moment to end. I whispered back, 'I love you.'

Now, alone with my memory, I grabbed my jacket and staggered into the garden for a few minutes of reflection and for a temporary pause from breakfast and from life. I thought about my brave Carole. How was she this morning – resting, eating breakfast, probably very sleepy? I wondered how she was coping. What were her thought processes and were her new drugs working? I had to believe she was OK as I pictured her in her hospital room sitting up in bed with toast and coffee watching TV. The tears streamed for a few more lonely seconds down my cheek before bouncing off my wax jacket onto the gravel path that crept around the side of the house.

A little voice called from the lounge, 'Dad! What's for breakfast?' bringing me back to my senses. 'What's for breakfast' was, I think, code for 'Where's my breakfast?' Breakfast was promptly delivered, albeit a few minutes late.

I had accepted my family's temporary departure from our normal operating standards, although I didn't like it for a single second. I feared everything it represented. Over the last weekend, there had been so many changes just in Carole's general demeanour, let alone anything else. It had become obvious our lives would have to change continuously from this point onward – day by day, maybe hour by hour. We would have to be reactive, adapt, and flex constantly just to cling on to enough control to maintain buoyancy of the most important things. Perhaps this was no longer about control but more now about management.

Carole and I knew that one day all four of us would need to dig deeply within ourselves and summon every ounce of courage to face our own destinies. The mere thought of Carole's destiny was unbearable. For her to accept it and understand it took immense inner strength. I had to find a way to cope with the harshest of emotional consequences to our children's world. Our ultimate nightmare was inching, I sensed, a little nearer now with every passing day. Maybe my memory that morning of Carole in the kitchen was telling me that she had started to dig deep. Carole's words echoed in my head: 'You will always be there for me.' Inspiration enough whenever I needed it to get me through the next few hours of any day. I needed it that morning.

With breakfast out of the way, the cat's litter tray cleaned, and the cat fed and watered, there was just enough time to stick some washing on. I quickly separated the whites from the colours and then the dark colours from the light colours and filled the washing machine before realising that there was no fabric conditioner. We'd run out! There were so many things to thinks about, to remember and to do.

Blokes don't multitask well – not this one, anyway. Note to self: get fabric conditioner. Other note to self: get better at this stuff. Fortunately, Carole's clean laundry was already complete for the week ahead, so no immediate panic. Some things, I was learning, would just have to wait.

Carole had been conditioning herself for the moment when she would feel the restlessness of her wings. This was something I know she agonised over silently every day for two years. The agony lay in not knowing. Carole talked often about trying to get to sleep each night with the uncertainty of what the next day would bring bouncing constantly and randomly around her aching head. Sometimes, our conversations about her innermost thoughts were short because, even for the bravest of hearts, it appeared that there was a pain threshold that simply rejected any further mental torture in the name of self-preservation. Throughout her illness, Carole was never sure that she would see tomorrow, and so she tried her best each evening, behind misty eyes, to sleep in the hope that she would. Carole would recount that it was such an incredible feeling to open her eyes every morning and remember who she was, where she was, and what she still had.

She would say, 'For this, I am so grateful.'

Ironically, her realisation and her relief that she lived to fight another day were stolen by a little fear when, within a silent heartbeat, her reality returned. As she progressed through illness, her little fear grew ever so slightly each day, as did her knowledge that in all probability her glioma was doing the same. In her own words, Carole would say lovingly that 'you don't know what it's like, Bun, to never know if you will ever open your eyes again.' At the same time, she remarked that 'I say this not because you don't understand, because you do, it's just that it's on my mind all the time – all the time.'

Carole was always grateful, and she always had hope. Every morning that she opened her eyes and orientated herself invoked a warm smile. It was the sort of smile that started deep within and radiated to touch the hearts of those she loved. She smiled because she knew she was alive, and to be alive meant one more day. She had one more day. One more day always felt like Christmas to Carole, and the present she unwrapped every morning with excitement and gratitude was another day with her family, with her children. My gift was Carole's presence of mind when I opened my eyes to that smile.

For all of us, everyday life with Carole was like a million Christmas Days all rolled into one, and the only gift we ever needed, ever wanted, and always cherished was one more day every day. Maybe that's why today is called the present, because to the four of us that's exactly what it was. We all valued our todays, and each one we were gifted to spend with Mummy was even more special than the one before, and all our yesterdays were the most special days in the whole world. They were the most special days because we knew that one day our yesterdays would be our memories as our tangible morphed silently into the intangible. I cry every time I think about those days. I wish we had just one more day to touch, to share, to talk, to hold hands, to laugh and listen and love, to care for each other and our children together in the fairy tale we were lucky enough to call our life.

The overwhelming sadness of the news just seven days before did the one thing I had been dreading. It devastated us. When I think back to the day we were told that Carole was terminally ill and learned about her life expectancy, it always feels like we were cheated from a lifetime of family, of happiness, and of love. Our consolation, if there was such a thing, was that we'd been given a second chance on that August day in 2009. We had a second chance to have another two and a quarter years to love Carole and to share in the life of a lovely Mummy and friend. More poignantly, Carole had a second chance to love and care for her children.

Carole had now begun the final leg of her journey. There was nothing anyone or anything could do about it. A powerful force and an unstoppable chain of events had started, and the mind-numbing uncertainty of when it would finish nobody knew. We were borrowing time.

For the past week, I had closed my eyes every evening never quite knowing what the next day would bring but safe in the knowledge that I would see it. I tried to imagine Carole's loneliness. What were her innermost thoughts – perhaps of her own loss, maybe of her grief for us? Did she have a sense of love and grief for herself in the knowledge that everything she held so dear would one day evaporate without permission, rhyme, or reason? These thoughts would be cruel for her and for the people she'd have to leave behind. Carole would feel the burden of both cruelties, because that is who she was. She was brave, and she smiled through all of these things.

People would often say to her, 'I don't know how you cope, Carole.'

Her reply was always the same. 'It is what it is. Things could be a lot worse.'

This was a reply that always managed to leave its recipients with much to think about – which, of course, was Carole's sole intention. Perhaps my memory that morning of Carole's loveliness was perfectly timed to get me through a few more hours when I needed her most. Maybe it was simply the magic of her weave sewn into the fabric of my consciousness showing me that help could be found within whenever I needed her most. Whatever it was, it was beautiful.

Carole had been away from us in hospital for a whole week, which felt like a month, a lifetime, or longer. The children and I were looking forward to getting Mummy home at some point over the next few days. To be together as a family within the safety of our little universe, our home, was all that we wanted.

I had started to think about some important and very special preparations for our last Christmas together … *our last Christmas together.* Even now as I commit these words to paper, it is unreal to think them, and to see them written in black and white feels like nothing I can describe. Christmas 2011 was one of our short-term milestones, and Carole would have been aware of this. In recent days, this particular milestone had been the driving force to push on through all weathers. It was my little rainbow of hope. There was so much to do and to organise, plan, and enjoy alongside any additional treatment and care that Carole would need.

Christmas was always going to be different, but we'd try to retain as much normality as possible without making things too special. *Too special* would mean too different, and too different would emphasize finality. We'd try to do what Carole had done for us over the period of her illness by keeping as much balance and normality in our lives as possible. Carole wanted a normal Christmas, and we would give her exactly what she wanted: nothing more, nothing less, and no fuss. It would be special for so many reasons anyway, and even though it was important that these reasons were acknowledged, it was equally important not to overplay them. This was going to be tough for Carole and not least of all the children. I had no idea how we would get through this, but I had a firm belief that together we would. It was time, once more, to live unconditionally in the moment.

Christmas was always Carole's favourite time of year. She would immerse herself wholeheartedly in festive fun and frivolity. She'd make lists, buy presents, and wrap presents lovingly with ribbon and bow. She hid presents sometimes and then forgot where she'd put them. Forgetting where she put them – perhaps another one of life's subtle ironies, knowing now that her memory was often unreliable. She'd never really grasped the significance of this until later in her life.

For at least the last ten years of our married life, Carole and I had taken time out together to spend two days Christmas shopping. This usually took place at the beginning of December. We'd quietly canvass the children to find out what their hearts desired and then trawl the shops to find their presents. We'd travel just a few miles to the quaint town of Royal Windsor in Berkshire to buy special gifts for urgent dispatch to Father Christmas and his elves.

It had become tradition on these days to take time out for a lunch break at Carole's favourite pizza restaurant. I was always grateful to rest weary legs, creased fingers, and my longer than usual arms, which felt like they'd stretched under the sheer weight of shopping bags. We'd spend about thirty minutes in pizza and fizzy water heaven replanning the afternoon's activities, checking and double-checking our list of essential items. Over the last two years, it had become a challenge to spend all day shopping, as drugs and fatigue crept exponentially into Carole's daily life. Despite this, her deep-rooted enthusiasm for these two special days never dwindled.

During our retail expedition of 2010, we were forced to cut short our day when Carole suffered a tonic-clonic seizure in the restroom at the pizza restaurant. She had been away from the table longer than usual, so naturally I went to see if she was OK. I found her in mid-seizure, gasping for air, crawling on her hands and knees up the stairs from the basement facilities. No one had stopped to help her. That particular seizure was a nasty one and so severe that I feared for Carole's ability to stay conscious. It took twenty-five long minutes for her to recover sufficiently to walk unaided.

During those everlasting minutes, all Carole could manage to say through her breathlessness was, 'I'm OK. I'm OK – I'm fine. Don't worry.'

The episode of illness in the restaurant that year motivated her to complete a full day's shopping, with more pizza, the following day. She collapsed on the sofa in a heap of presents when we got home safely at the end of day two and exclaimed, 'We did it, Bun, we did it!'

Christmas was always the time of year when Carole was her truest self. Her radiant spark elevated our excitement and enthusiasm, and usually everyone else's wherever she went. I desperately wanted Carole to have one final festive foray of retail therapy and pizza.

The first Sunday in December was always the day we put up the family Christmas tree in the lounge. This was a tradition we'd maintained since becoming parents. In her own unique way, Carole decorated the Christmas tree with delicate simplicity and artistic precision. Gold ribbons and crimson bows, flowers, baubles, and curly twizzle sticks were all arranged thoughtfully against a night-time glow of white twinkling fairy lights. The same gold trumpet-blowing angel occupied the highest point each year, positioned deftly by Carole before we switched the lights on.

A daily inspection of the tree ensured decorations were maintained to Carole's exacting standards. She had an eye for detail and a magical touch. On many a winter's night, after the children had gone to bed, we'd sit together on the sofa with only the flicker of an open fire and soft twinkling white lights for company. This was Carole's idea of Christmas heaven.

The month of Christmas really started for us on 1 December every year when Carole wrapped up an advent calendar for each of the children. She'd pop a gift tag on each one with the same handwritten message that she would scrawl with her left hand to disguise her own handwriting. The note simply said, 'Happy Christmas with love from the elves,' followed by three kisses. Carole bought the calendars for the children and I provided one for her, always with the same simple message, a ribbon, and a bow. I would write the same message on her gift tag with my left hand too.

Carole's unique brand of Christmas spirit transformed our house into a wonderful festive cottage, with seasonal decorations in every downstairs room. The candle shimmer of fairy lights, the diamond sparkle in her eyes, and the winter sunshine of her smile lit up our family home on the coldest of Christmas days and nights. Every Christmas Eve, Carole tucked the children up in their beds and read to them 'Twas the Night before Christmas.' This never failed to fuel an air of excitement and surprise. The children loved it too.

In December 2011, we longed to be her autumn leaves, her winter sunshine, her snowy blanket, and her three kisses. We'd keep her safe and warm as best we could in the contented winter of her life. We had so much to look forward to. One day, we'd have so much to look back on too. I had wanted Carole home as soon as possible so that together we could make the best normal Christmas for everyone. Besides, she had a tree to decorate!

The children got themselves ready for school. I'd emptied the dishwasher, had a quick tidy up, and got myself ready. We left the house at approximately eight fifteen and drove the short distance to school. As we listened to the radio, I updated the children as I'd done at this time for the past week. I let them know about my activities for the day and the evening's arrangements for them to see Mummy.

That morning, I dropped them off, kissed them both twice, and sent them onward to face one more day of difference with lots of love from both of us. I watched them walk together for a few seconds chatting casually to each other as they went. The fabric of my heart tore out of love for their resolve and their friendship for each other. Watching them walk away, I had another one of those moments that make you stop and think about life and just how beautiful and fragile it really is. Love was the fragile catalyst sparking a beautifully emotional moment that told me how lucky I was.

I drove away thinking about the schedule ahead of me. The car's digital dashboard flashed and then beeped high-pitch. I needed petrol. A slight detour was needed before I started my journey to Carole. I'd forgotten to get petrol the previous evening – just too many things to juggle, to organise, and remember. Carole would have reminded to get petrol! I'd have to get much better at doing this stuff.

My head hurt and I felt sick. Carole's head hurt every day. My problems were nothing compared to Carole's daily struggle to simply function, breathe, wash, eat, sleep, rest, and remember. There was just so much stuff going round in my head, and it was on my mind all the time.

I popped into the local garage that Carole and I had bought petrol from for many a year. Hazel's larger-than-life smile greeted me when I went to pay. Hazel was one of the garage's cashiers, and we'd always chat for a few minutes while she processed my transaction. She was a lovely, jolly, down-to-earth character with a happy heartfelt smile and a humour light-of-foot for any journey, any day. That day, like all days, she made me smile.

Petrol purchased, and almost back on schedule, I let my thoughts drift back to events of the weekend during my private visit with Carole on Saturday and again with the children on Sunday afternoon. It was obvious to me that there'd been a decline in Carole's ability to recall aspects of our life together. Events, people, and chronology were absent and confused. I wondered if her emotional and sensory connections to these memories were also lost. Maybe they were locked in temporary suspension somewhere in the recesses of her mind.

Perhaps I could again rebuild the temporal pathways to her memory through my own emotional and pseudo-sensory account of her missing years. I hoped that we could do this together one day. I'd bounced many different scenarios around my head, and each one arrived delicately to the same horizon of conclusion.

Carole had lost some weight over the past week or so, and despite her cheery and smiley resolve, she was not in terribly good physical shape. Pastier than usual and a little gaunt, she'd lost all interest in food, and even her dainty thin-rimmed reading glasses had looked heavy for her cadaverous face. On Saturday, I'd chatted privately with the pink nurse about Carole's general well-being and was casually advised that invasive brain surgery was planned for Tuesday. Tuesday was now the next day.

The pressure inside Carole's head had become dangerously high due to a very rapid expansion of the glioma. As the sticky pancake grew, it invaded space already occupied by normal tissue. Pain and mental deterioration were, therefore, heart-breakingly inevitable. For my own sanity's sake I needed to know the details.

I'd taken no part in any discussion with Carole or the medical team about surgery. A natural anxiety overwhelmed me in the car as it had during the previous evening's insomnia. I wondered if Carole knew what was happening. Her head was filling beyond bearable capacity.

On Saturday, I'd tackled the difficult question of what might be at sea as we sailed into the big blue beyond. Carole's memory had been sketchy at best. The information I needed was no longer flowing. It felt, at times, like we were both swimming against the tide, caught on banks of moving sand and unforgiving undercurrents. There was a danger that somehow we'd be shipwrecked and lost in the translation of our inner fears and inflected emotion. Either Carole couldn't recall conversations and vital information or she'd deliberately avoided what would be for both of us another course of painful navigation. Perhaps it was a bit of both things.

Her response to my questions was simply, 'Oh! I don't know, Bun!'

On the basis that Carole had always been a sharp, straight-talking, 'bring it on' kind of girl, my natural assumption at the time was that her memory had simply failed her. I think this is what she may have wanted me to think. I now believe she had been doing what she did at her brilliant best every day. She was protecting us. She was protecting herself. She was protecting me.

Carole had most likely made the toughest decision of her life which, in all probability, would have only one destination. As she did this, she was throwing me her life jacket, her lifeline. Carole remained fearlessly at the helm of her ship as destiny softly whispered her name through candyfloss clouds of indigo and orange.

My instincts and my heart were showing me that Carole had charted a solo course in her determined mind. This was her unspoken wish. Her life listing gently to starboard, perhaps quietly guided by Venus herself, Carole had set the sails and was slowly heading out on a calm, shimmering, mercurial sea into the diamond sunset of her mortal life. It goes without saying how I felt about her. How I will always feel about her.

On Sunday, Carole had not known my name. She knew I was her husband, that she loved me, and that I was the father of her children. She confused my nationality. She knew that we were married, had spent eighteen years together, but she didn't know my name. Even though her eyes never lost their sparkle, they let me know on Sunday evening, with peaceful beauty, all that I needed to know, feel, and see. That was the defining moment when I realised I was beginning to lose my fairy tale princess.

The world we'd created for our children was a naturally balanced one, and one filled with love. Even though it was a world of duality, of opposites, of sunshine and rain, of attraction and distraction and of so many other beautiful things, it was always balanced. I knew that balance would be key in the days and months ahead.

Carole and I were beginning to take separate journeys, and she'd conditioned me, almost subliminally, to accept this. Her words 'This could be much worse' bought temporary relief from fear and put perspective to the unthinkable and the unimaginable. Upon her maiden voyage, Carole was herself the influence that calmed her seas, made haste the winds which cleared a path and beckoned an eternal sunset. Our life path was crossing these winds which carried beginnings, a heart of heavy water, and a soul of eternal sunshine.

Maybe, just maybe, there was a place somewhere out there under brightest moon of fantasy and light. A place where one day we could join up some more dots, paint rainbows together, and fly above the winds of change on the wings of love. The world my family knew was changing. It had entered its own phase of complex seizure. If only this could be simple and partial, I would know what to do.

I'd descended a little way down my ladder of emotions in the car, and this hit me hard. As I reached the motorway, all I could think about was the unknown, about Carole, her surgery and its immediacy. I decided to call the hospital. I got off the motorway and made the call. After just a few minutes, a meeting had been arranged. The time was not set, but I'd meet with the team that morning.

I also decided, there and then, that I needed to let school know about Carole's health. I have no idea why this was so important to me, but something was telling me it was time to pop in for a chat. I had learned to trust my instincts on my lovely journey through life with Carole. My heart and my instincts had never let me down, so I did what they asked.

It was at that point that reality took the wind out my sails again. It hit me so hard this time that my breathing quickened and my vision became blurred. My head went blank and fuzzy for a few seconds before the coldness of my temples bought me back to the driver's seat. I was scared. Not scared for me, but for my three best friends.

Carole and I had decided back in August 2009 that we wouldn't hide anything from our children. We tried hard to find language that didn't worry them too much about what was happening to Mummy. To this day, I am entirely sure that we did the right thing.

It was our collective and steadfast agreement to do this despite the inner torment and the strength and mindfulness that would be needed. The inner torment was worth the effort, as it had been, and continues to be, so instrumental in maintaining the stability of family life.

The other thing we'd agreed on together, with nothing but absolute certainty, was that everyday life for the children was to be kept as normal as normal could be. What this actually meant was that we would only reveal Carole's condition to a handful of people, including our nearest and dearest. Above all else, we wanted the children's school life to be normal. 'Normal' to us was a place they could go every day and behave, act, and socialise with their peer groups without bumping into things that would make them feel different or test their mettle.

On this basis, we'd decided not to tell the children's school about Carole's illness. The children were free to tell anyone they wanted, but there was to be no formal communication to the school until it was necessary. Carole was very insistent on that point. It was what she wanted, and it goes without saying that I trusted her maternal wisdom.

Sometimes you have to find a way that meets your needs regardless of what anyone else thinks. When you care too much about what people think, you can lose your identity quite innocently for all the right reasons – or reasons which appear to be right at the time. We were ever mindful of others, but we never lost our identity as a family unit to do things that we had decided to do to get us through life one day at a time. The four of us did whatever felt right, and we never stopped talking to each other. We were able to do this because we knew ourselves and each other. We also knew that one day this would be a source of strength and inspiration for all of us.

The school receptionist called me back very quickly to let me know that a meeting with the appropriate personnel had been arranged for approximately two thirty that afternoon. I sobbed in the car after calling the school because I knew that making that call had deep meaning. Out of meaning was driven the necessity from which reality prevailed.

I rejoined the motorway traffic with a new itinerary whizzing inside my head. While I drove, I tried to map things together into a new schedule. The key to everything working was the appointment at the hospital, so I'd have to manage that time proactively upon arrival. It was all doable. It all slotted nicely into place, and I wondered, for the remainder of my journey, how this had come to be.

Traffic was unusually quiet, and the journey into London had been straightforward. I was excited and anxious and didn't really know what to expect. I forced myself to keep an open mind and a crystal-clear focus on what I would hear, see, and feel.

I'd somehow managed to live my life to this point in the real world, although life had taught me that *real* means different things to different people at different times in their lives. Real is sometimes a place where reality and illusion become confused according to thought, environmental conditions, need, and perspective. The vantage point I'd adopted to look after my family over the years had provided a solid footing to observe all manner of things. I suppose I was a sort of a pessimistic optimist – someone who expected the worst sometimes, when necessary, so that if outcomes improved beyond worst-case my reality was a pleasant surprise. I guess this was just another form of self-preservation – better to be surprised occasionally than let down all the time. This let me float up into the clouds from time to time too, although my feet usually stayed on the ground.

On those occasions I escaped the shackles of terra firma, I knew I could rely on Carole to ground me. She had an endearing charm that shone through her subtle, often directly matter-of-fact but always honest way of telling me that I'd strayed too far from her safety. She had a code word, just one word, which always brought me tumbling back with a bump. It wasn't an unkind word but one that managed to stop me in my tracks every time. It compelled me to grasp the round ornamental handle that opened the door to the sea of inner-me. Sometimes just her smile, a funny face, a quirky eye-rolling grin, or some raised eyebrows was all it took.

I drew strength from the fact that Carole and I had grown together to become naturally objective people; we were usually very measured in our collaborative understanding of most things, especially each other. That morning, I had to find a way to be measured in my understanding of Carole's illness and its peripheral effects on all of us. The rate of Carole's deterioration over the last weekend had meant that perhaps she was unable now to be my assurance – the voice outside my head. My level-headed companion was, quite literally, taking her leave of absence. I resigned myself to fate and let the 'everything happens for a reason' blanket of life wrap itself around Carole and I once more. Given my recent conversations with the pink nurse, it was all I could do.

I fought hard with my inner self to be positive about the next few hours. I had a bloody good cry in the car, and then I told myself to stop being a circular ornamental door handle. I arrived at the hospital and, surprisingly, found a parking space very quickly. The day was getting more unusual by the hour.

At Carole's bedside, I found her fast asleep and a picture of loveliness in her fluffy white dressing gown patterned in two-tone blue hearts. She lay propped up against several pillows and was covered snugly in her white cotton bedding and a blue woven blanket. I sat quietly and held her warm fragile hand for twenty minutes. I lovingly observed the soft contours of her freckly face as I etched them to memory for the millionth time.

Carole woke naturally from her nap and acknowledged my presence. She didn't call me by my name. She knew I was her husband, but she didn't know my name – not even the fluffy nickname she had affectionately given me. I didn't care in that moment, because she simply smiled and extended her arms for a hug. She always gave wonderful hugs, the sort of hugs that let you know you were deeply loved.

She asked me about our children. This too was wonderful, because in her own kafuffled way that meant she did actually know who I was. I remarked, 'It's nice to know that you know who I am today.'

She replied, 'But how do I really know that I'm talking to you?'

My heart melted and my eyes streamed, because in Carole-speak what she was actually trying to tell me was that she might not know who I was over the next few days. Carole was thinking ahead. Again, her words helped me to appreciate that she was still in control, still thinking and being selfless. It was so much more than this, because what she was actually doing was gently wrapping the winds of change around the two of us before they carried us lovingly in different directions.

A little moment of spontaneous magic followed when I suggested to Carole, 'Ask me a question about your feet so then you'll know it's me.'

She said, 'Do you like my feet?'

I gave the same honest answer that I always did in reply: 'No! I hate your feet!'

Carole smiled through her pain and simply said, 'Now I know I am talking to you!' We both laughed as best we could behind the waterfall of tears we now streamed together. In a moment of beautiful togetherness, our tears fell perfectly upon the sensual lips of a kiss for all seasons that sealed us as one in our ocean of love.

She said, 'I might not know what your bloody name is, but I know I love you.'

Carole only remembered me from that point onward as the guy who hated her feet! I enjoyed proving to her several times more that I was indeed her guy. We chatted about how she was feeling and the usual stuff couples talk about, and even though conversation felt different, we managed to keep it in full flow for the few hours we spent together before I had to leave to pick up the children. We didn't talk about illness – we didn't have to. It was lovely to have the opportunity to just sit and talk with my best friend. It was lovely because time was slowing down. Time was breaking my heart.

A steady flow of nurses popped in and out to perform routine observations, to give Carole her drugs, and just to check on her general condition. All the nurses were chatty and lovely, every one of them an angel. Some of them spoke softly while others spoke with raised voices, thinking that Carole couldn't hear them! I learned that Carole hadn't eaten much breakfast, which meant that her industrial-strength meds might unsettle her stomach. Lunch was being wheeled around the ward, and as Carole's arrived she was encouraged to eat.

Always on the lookout for an opportunity to have fun, I decided to inject some humour into the challenge of getting Carole to eat something. We reminisced about how we used to play the aeroplane game at mealtimes with our babies when we tried to sneak new foods under their taste and smell radars. It was lovely because Carole recalled those times. She was able to describe a red plastic spoon and a blue and white Winnie the Pooh bowl and plate. She was also able to tell me that the bowl and plate still occupied space in a kitchen cupboard at home. We played aeroplanes for a while, with sound effects and shared laughter, until it was just too much for her to stomach.

Carole's bedside cabinet was stocked with her favourite snack foods, so we managed to supplement her main meal with a few mouthfuls of favourite confectionary and chocolate. There were times during lunch when she just stopped conversation mid-sentence and stared at her surroundings and at me as if to say 'Who are you and why are you trying to feed me?' before returning to knowing where she was. The main thing was that Carole had eaten something.

Not long after lunch, Mr White arrived on the ward and popped in to see Carole. He had a short conversation with her. She recognised him and knew his name. I asked Carole if she could tell Mr White what her name was, which she did. I asked her where she lived, which she knew, and then I asked her what my name was. Carole couldn't recall this detail, at which point Mr White turned to me and said, 'Let's go and have a chat.' I kissed Carole and let her know that I'd be back soon.

We walked to a small room just a few steps away on the opposite side of the ward corridor and sat down with a few members of Carole's lovely team. Rhetorically, Mr White said, 'She's deteriorated quite a lot, hasn't she?' I asked for a quick update on Carole's condition. In particular, I wanted to understand the changes to her glioma and the options being considered for surgery.

I was taken on a small journey over the next five or ten minutes. It was the news that no husband ever wants to hear. In my heart, I already knew, but to hear someone else speak these words was tough: 'The growth of the tumour over the past week has been very aggressive, and radio therapy and chemotherapy are no longer viable.'

I just went stone cold, fuzzy and blank again. This signalled that the initial three-month best-case guestimate for Carole's life expectancy, conveyed just seven days ago, was no longer in play. All I could think about was Carole and the children, but I had to listen to every word.

Our plans for Christmas were now in tatters. I wondered if Carole was aware of her situation. What would I tell the children? What did all this really mean? I sat there sinking inwardly. It was calm. I felt so sick.

Mr White went on to say that as the glioma continued to grow rapidly, there was no space for it to grow into. The pressure in Carole's head was therefore dangerously high, and this was causing deterioration of brain functionality and much discomfort to Carole. Deterioration was now very visible externally. To relieve the pressure, urgent surgical intervention was needed. Tuesday was mentioned.

We talked about the surgical options. The first was to perform minor surgery. This would relieve pressure via a small biopsy. A biopsy carried high risk of the removal of normal brain tissue due to the sticky blurred-line fusion of bad tissue to good. The second option was major surgery to remove a vast amount of tumour. I imagined this to be equal to at least a quarter of Carole's brain, maybe a lot more. With major surgery, of course, there existed major risk.

I listened as the outcome of my wife's beautiful life was professionally and compassionately put to me in a language I could understand. I wanted to scream. I wanted Carole to hug me and tell me everything would be OK.

Mr White continued, 'With major surgery, there would be no alternative but to sever the connection between the left and right sides of Carole's brain. To sever the left and right sides would permanently disconnect the thinking side of her brain from the doing side of her brain.'

I held it together long enough to process what had just been said. All I was concerned about was Carole's quality of life. I imagined machines and tubes and lifelessness that would serve no purpose other than to delay the inevitable. More importantly, I believed that major surgery would cause Carole incredible distress and discomfort, and I knew that if she was in any way conscious of this, she would never forgive me – and I would never forgive myself. I was thinking about the children too.

In my mind, I had eliminated major surgery at that juncture of the conversation. I wrestled to retain my composure and somehow played back to the team of watery-eyed professionals my understanding of the surgical options for Carole. I was also thinking about a third option.

In the next few minutes, I took the team on a difficult journey through a set of thought processes and my understanding. I wanted us to reach consensus. My heart was broken, but we had to have the conversation. I played back the surgical options. Minor surgery had significant risks, and there was no guarantee of improvement in quality of life or life expectancy. Major surgery carried serious risk with a guarantee of rapid deterioration. I talked through my third option, and we arrived together at the same conclusion. I paused from our journey of thoughts and looked around the silent room for some sign of hope.

I found myself in the place I had feared most. No one could help me, but more importantly, I realised no one could help Carole. I wanted to scream and shout so much, to kick something, to do something. What good would it do? I knew that in the next moment, I was the only person who could make the hardest decision for my lovely wife. What would Carole do? What would she want?

My memory of Carole's words on that fateful morning filled my head for the second time on that day. Her words, her voice, in the kitchen when I caught her staring at me with sun-kissed face during softest whisper of the most beautiful words, 'I know you will always be there for me.' I knew what she wanted. My heart glowed in the presence of her thought and emotional surrender of love in the moment. Carole had said the only thing that she had ever needed to say, and that was, 'I trust you to do the right thing, and as hard as it will be, you will know what to do.' Carole had trusted me with her life. It was that time most horrible to prove her trust of me in perhaps the most loving but toughest way imaginable.

Carole had endured the most terrible things on her journey through illness. She had fought so hard to stay, so bravely to love, and so courageously to smile through everything, every seizure, through the unconscious moments when her life had tilted precariously between life and life ever after. There were no more second chances, and we'd raided the bank of tomorrows, I sensed, for perhaps the last time.

I searched the faces of the people with me one last time. In quick summary, I recapped, 'So, if minor or major surgery can't provide any positive outcomes to either Carole's quality of life or her life expectancy, then to do nothing gives us the same outcomes?'

Yes was the answer I received.

It was the answer I had anticipated but didn't want to hear. I didn't want to hear it, because in that moment I was about to do the hardest thing I've ever done. The next few minutes passed in slow motion. I knew what I had to do. Saying it was tough. Understanding it was tougher. I opened my heart unconditionally and let love fly to my love.

Mr White simply said, 'We need to know now what you would like us to do.'

'If we do nothing, then palliative care is where our efforts will be focused?' was my final question.

Yes was the answer as the team exchanged silent glances with each other before fixing their gaze back on me. The words that followed, I spoke softly and slowly.

'Carole doesn't want to suffer for any greater period than is necessary unless there is hope of improving her situation. That hope is now gone, and so now we have to make sure that Carole is pain-free and as comfortable as she can be.' I paused, and then I trusted Carole's trust in me. 'I don't want you to perform any surgery. Carole does not want this.'

I had my consensus and reached it, I think, in the only way possible. We did that with love. I thanked the team and left them discussing next steps. I walked the few squeaky paces back across the corridor to Carole's room. It was the longest and loneliest walk. My internal scream was silent.

My beautiful girl was sleeping. I sat and stared at Carole's face for a few minutes and cried quietly so as not to wake her. Sunshine lit up her room while we shared moments unspoken. I held her hand and closed my eyes. In my bruised heart, I sensed that a rare and very beautiful butterfly was flapping her restless wings in preparation for flight.

For the first time, my fear was tangible. I knew this because it shook me to my core and then it shook me some more. I couldn't stop shaking. It was another one of those deep and unexpected feelings that ignites a spark of hope somewhere in the bowels of reality. It's that kind of unmistakeable feeling that somehow defies explanation until all finally becomes clear after long periods of stone-cold reflection. It's the kind of feeling that never really ever goes away, day after day, but instead returns slowly to its hiding place, only to resurface unexpectedly and remind us of its presence from time to time.

I suppose that you could liken this in some ways to the sensation of an epileptic seizure. You know it's there, it's invasive, it waits, and then a chemical-like intoxication overwhelms before the natural calmness which always follows. When Carole had seizure-free periods throughout her illness, she used to say that she missed her seizures because they had become her friends. They were part of each other and never apart. I used to wonder what she was trying to tell me, as she often struggled through her kafuffledness to find the right words to reflect her thoughts. But in our moment unspoken I knew exactly what she felt.

I tried desperately to turn my attention to other things. With each gentle flutter, my stomach let me know that I was sinking deeper and deeper in the sea of love. I knew I was drowning, but there were no gasps for air. For moments I was trapped in the womb of fear with nowhere to go. Behind my eyes it was dark, but I could see everything. The only sound was the muffled echo of a pulsating drum beating and fading through the soft-walled recesses of my self-imposed confinement. I was floating. Then there was the forcefulness of pain, followed by an overwhelming sense of warmth, like being wrapped in a duvet of sunset clouds that were made manifest by Carole's love.

Time was short, and I was grateful to find Carole peacefully asleep so that she couldn't see my face or hear the incoherence of my speech. I was unable to control the rush of adrenaline. I kissed her forehead very gently, just above her eyes as she always liked. I whispered of love's softness to my elemental princess and kissed her once more. I let the hospital staff know that I'd be back later and ran with piggy eyes to the sanctuary of my car. School was the next stop. I didn't want to leave Carole, but I knew she wanted to see her children and I knew they wanted to see their Mum. Had Carole been awake, she'd have simply dispatched me to return with them post-haste. I sensed that time was of her essence.

Travelling the M25 was always an interesting experience, usually with stop-start traffic and variable speed restrictions designed to keep traffic on the move. I was grateful that afternoon for the constant speed of safe passage back to Berkshire. It gave me time to be alone, to grieve again privately. I cried all the way. I cried for Carole. I cried for our children. I cried for our family of four best friends. Our brave journey into the unknown had started.

For three of us, this journey would be very different, but we'd make sure it was balanced. Carole was in a sort of transition, as though an unexplainable but natural process had started to guide her home. Maybe it was something else. Maybe it was simply that Carole had found deepest inner peace and this was the lasting piece that completed the jigsaw of her life. My Carole – the quintessential ordinary girl who couldn't make a cup of tea but made love her only ambition in life.

I popped back home for ten quick minutes, freshened up, and changed my shirt before arriving not terribly composed at school. I didn't have to wait long, just a few minutes. In those minutes, I gathered my thoughts and prepared for a difficult conversation. I set the scene and explained that Carole had been ill for some time and that, as parents, we'd tried to retain some normality of life for our children throughout. It had been so important to us to maintain this as best as possible, and Carole and I had taken the perhaps unusual step of not letting school know for this reason.

The teachers and I had a lovely and very professional conversation, during which I also outlined the near-time probability of taking the children out of school at short notice and without explanation. This was understood. As our meeting closed, I thanked both heads of year for their time and their support of our children, and for the ongoing support of the school. I jumped back in the car just as my emotions got the better of me again. I drove straight home, slightly ahead of schedule, to freshen up once more before collecting our little ones and going to see Mummy.

After collecting the children from school, I whizzed back home so they too could freshen up. My daughter grabbed her GCSE revision material while I pulled together a collection of our favourite sweets and chocolates, some brioche, cartons of apple juice, and some bottled water. We headed back into London as rush hour approached. Our journey this time was not as easy, as weather conditions deteriorated very quickly under a torrent of unrelenting rain. I was at one with nature for a while. The M25 was unforgiving, as we hit mile upon mile of slow-moving traffic.

Conditions delayed us by just over an hour and a half. The children were super-patient and kept in touch by text message with Carole's parents, who had been at her bedside during the afternoon. We learned that Mummy was very sleepy and that she'd been moved from her side room onto the main ward. Visiting time at the hospital finished at eight o'clock, and we finally arrived at Carole's bedside just before seven. Carole's Mum and Dad had let Carole know that we were on our way and that we'd been caught in traffic. Carole had given her Mum a message for us just in case we weren't able to get to the hospital in time. The message was 'always three kisses'. Carole was still one move ahead, caring and protecting.

The ward lights were low, as were the voices of staff, patients, and visitors. The curtains around Carole's bed were drawn on either side. She was struggling to support herself and sit upright, and it was difficult for her to open her eyes. Speech was soft and controlled. Carole knew that we were all there. It was obvious to me that she found herself in an unfamiliar place – the place that she had fought so hard to resist for so long. For the first time throughout her illness, Carole looked very poorly. In typical Carole style, she fashioned the most beautiful smile, which invoked so many lovely emotions.

There was something very different about her that evening. It wasn't that she looked ill or was weaker than she'd ever been in her life. It wasn't that she needed almost constant supervision from the team of nurses who were now so very concerned about her that during the next hour there was always one of them at her side. What was different now was the exaggerated softness in her voice, the sunshine warmth, the sensitivity and deliberation of her every word, and the amplified gentleness of every fragile movement.

Carole was angelic. Her heart was doing her thinking for her, more so than it always had. She was ever fearless. Across our sentient bridge, Carole's heart was breaking silently. The layers of self-styled titanium armour had vanished. I saw Carole in all her vulnerability, just as I had for every day of our life together. I held her hand and sensed the brush of quickening in her wings.

It is difficult to define love sometimes. All I can say is that just when you think the love you have for someone so very special to you can't ever be surpassed, exceeded, or bettered in any way, when you know you can't love your partner any more than is physically and emotionally possible, be prepared to be amazed. Carole always amazed me, not just through her illness but throughout our life together. She calmly found solutions for every problem or puzzle, whether it be the merits of a correctly re-stacked dishwasher, what to cook for tea, her thoughtful and humorous resolution of poor service in a restaurant, or even her ability to suppress a seizure through self-infliction of excruciating physical pain. She amazed me again as I watched her now with our children for a few incredibly moving minutes. Despite everything happening to her, Carole found the strength to ignore her fragility, her vulnerability, and her fatigue so that she could just be Mummy to the most special people in her world, in a beautiful and extraordinary moment shared between three ordinary and very beautiful people. Their bond of friendship was unbreakable.

Just when I thought I'd hit the ceiling of capacity and understanding of my love for Carole, there she was taking it up to another level, transcending anything I'd ever felt. Carole was a simple and ordinary lady of remarkable substance and humanity. She was all these things because she was a woman and a mother. She was a mother who simply loved her children and her life.

The medical team needed to give Carole some attention, so the three of us decided to take a short break, and we sat together in the ward corridor for a while. The children were, I think, unaware of the potential seriousness of our situation. I decided to leave it that way for the time being.

I managed to get a sliver of time with the green nurse before visiting time ended, and we talked frankly for a few minutes. I learned that Carole was completely aware of everything happening to her. She was aware of everything. I understood everything that I ever needed to know. I decided that I couldn't share my knowledge with anyone and worked hard mentally to process the one thing that Carole and I together had feared most of all. I used one of Carole's gifts to do this. I used Carole's gift of acceptance. I couldn't do anything else. I searched my soul for inspiration and I found it. I found a flutter and a song. I found Carole.

The three of us were able to pop back to see Mummy momentarily to say goodnight. I grabbed a private moment with Carole while the green nurse occupied the children with general conversation in the ward corridor. At a shadowy and peaceful bedside, Carole and I managed to bravely exchange, understand, and decode two very simple but deeply meaningful and incredibly moving messages. We used the same uncomplicated and unfrightening language that we'd used together to guide our children through the minefield of life made difficult by epilepsy and tumour.

It was time again for medication, and I helped Carole take her pain-killing tablets, guiding very gently a small paper cup of water to her trembling left hand and then on to her parched but beautiful lips.

Carole had her eyes closed and whispered, 'What about the children? What about the children?'

This was Carole's way of saying that she was unsure how long she could continue to fight to stay with us. This was her way of seeking her own assurance that perhaps it was time for both of us to acknowledge this safely.

I reassured the love of my life as best I could, saying, 'Don't worry about the children, they will be fine, please don't worry. I'll look after them for you. See you tomorrow, my darling. I love you.'

These words flew without conscious thought. I somehow managed to choose words that would let Carole know that I knew what she was telling me. This was my way of saying *I know that you can't stay for much longer, my lovely, and regardless of everything in front of us we will be OK.* 'See you tomorrow, my darling – I love you' was my way of saying the hardest thing. I was saying farewell in my own way, in the knowledge that our tomorrow would never come. We were saying this to each other.

We shared a magical moment before Carole rested her head on the stack of pillows, and with eyes still closed she simply smiled and turned her head away from me. I whispered six words in her left ear. I asked her to promise me something. Carole's drugs were sending her to sleep. She was exhausted. I was again grateful that her eyes were closed.

The journey home was straightforward from a driving perspective, although there were some moments when it was difficult to stay awake at the wheel. The radio was on, the air con was on, and the driver's window was half open. We talked about all sorts of things during the hour it took to get us back safely in the darkness and the rain.

The children and I shared an hour or so in the lounge together and tried to relax as best we could before sleep. I spent a few minutes tidying up and secured the house before reaching for the sanctuary of Carole's pillows and my duvet. It was impossible to sleep. My insomnia companion was the mirrored stranger who, that evening, had no words. I streamed his tears and he wiped my face.

8

No Time to Stay

I awoke on Tuesday, 15 November 2011, to the usual sound of the alarm at six thirty. I did what I did every morning and hit the snooze button several times before remembering the urgency with which I'd reminded myself to wake up promptly the evening before. My sleep had been even more disturbed than usual, as I lay in bed until the very early hours thinking about our visit to see Carole in hospital the evening before.

The events of the previous day returned to haunt me upon waking. My eyes were itchy. I was exhausted. I guessed I'd had maybe three or four hours sleep at best. The decline in Carole's general health had itself caused alarm; intuitively, I knew everything I needed to know, and I was beside myself.

It was time to wake up the children and prepare them for another school day. Breakfast was eaten in front of the television after the usual early morning hustle and bustle, the queue for the bathroom, a packed lunch for one, dinner money for the other, and a quick run-through of our daily itinerary. I let the children know who was picking them up and about the arrangements for going to see Mummy after that. School bags were always packed the night before, ready for the following day. Carole had invested much time and effort to teach the children the importance of a properly pre-packed school bag, and both children had adopted a mature attitude and become competent self-managers in this regard.

It was another clockwork start to the day, with all of us playing our parts with consummate ease and understanding. On this particular morning, I had to drop my daughter off earlier than usual for an exam and then pop back home to collect my son and take him to school twenty minutes later.

I was a preoccupied with thoughts of Carole during both trips to school but tried hard to push these to one side during the few minutes in the car. Since waking that morning, I'd had the departing words of the green nurse the evening before whizzing randomly around my head, and they collided violently as I drove through the morning traffic. They bounced off one thought and then another and another without finding their way to an empty space in the congested cranial car park that was my head. I was driving my thoughts in circles – or maybe it was the other way around.

It had been suggested that I shouldn't rush into the hospital that morning. Instead, it was proposed that I should call the ward for an update on Carole's condition before starting my journey. The task of unravelling this remark into a rational context was impossible other than to accept it for what it was. My anxiety was growing, my concern was off the scale, and my ability to shackle all of my emotions deserted me on the way back from school for the second time. I pulled the car into the drive, switched off the engine, and just sat with head in hands and cried. I found myself consumed by a sense of overwhelming sadness. It was a powerful and very intense feeling that I'd never experienced before.

My heart sank as a vision of Carole sitting in her hospital bed floated into my consciousness. Collapsing and sinking to previously unexplored fathoms, I was drowning again in the womb of deepest fear. For a moment, I was unable to support myself and rested my forehead gently on the top of the steering wheel. Carole was looking frail and wore the same grimace across her face – the one caused by the duality of pain she felt for her and for us. Her eyes were closed.

I thought of the last words Carole had spoken to me the previous evening. I felt the love of her lips kissing me and the softness of her cheek on my fingertips. Her eyes, still closed, had dry white tear marks cascading from their outer corners. Her smile was gorgeous as she pressed her cheek hard to my hand, returning love spontaneously in the only way she could muster from her vulnerable and fragile form. She glowed in that moment. The dry tears had been on display all week to anyone observant enough to notice them.

I remembered the smile on Carole's face as we kissed each other. It was a smile that shone through challenge to create opportunity and was as natural and affectionate as ever. I fought hard to shepherd all my thoughts. My head was heavy and felt like it was about to explode. I thought of Carole. What would she do? How would she cope? Carole's head must have felt like it would explode on lots of days. The Carole I loved and adored would lose herself for a few moments, as I had done, and then she'd pick herself up, smile, accept the situation for what it was, and summon the deepest and strongest determination to carry on. I managed to regain just enough composure to get out of the car, lock it, and walk the short distance of gravel path to the front door.

I put the brass key in the tarnished lock and turned it, opened the door, and without thinking announced myself as I had always done.

'Carole, I'm ho—.'

I stopped mid-flow. My favourite photograph of Carole greeted me from its perch on the bookcase in the hall – and then it stopped me dead in my tracks. I was rooted to the spot about two feet away from the bottom of the stairs when my heart raced without warning. I couldn't breathe for a second. I was motionless but emotional. I cried like a child and was consumed by unfamiliar ice-like warmth. A lightness of body overcame the heaviness of thought, head, and heart. These feelings weren't in any way unpleasant, just so unexpected and out of the blue. I sensed I was not alone. Something was happening, but not just to me. Something was wrong, and I was powerless to stop it.

I have no idea why in that moment everything found gentle suspension. Even though I was cold and dizzy, a veil of calm and peaceful reassurance had descended. I was screaming 'No!' over and over again, but the words made no sound. They echoed silently in the lightest recesses of my universe where all that melted was the moment – the moment I had lived, enjoyed, and loved for eighteen years with the most beautiful of hearts as we swam together as one in the sea of love's perpetual embrace.

It felt like time was standing still in mournful delight at our moment of fulfilment, of happy times, of compassion, of love and for love. The wings of Carole's love brushed the fabric of my heart, ripping it gently with delicate precision and deeper incisions flutter by flutter. I was haemorrhaging and surrendering unconditionally to the quickening of wings and the crimson tide leaking ice into my chest and veins.

My vision was blurred. The noise in my ears was muffled. There was a bell ringing. I couldn't stop myself shaking. There was a powerful magnetic resonance and a pitch of perfection with each gently destructive movement of flight. In the blink of an eye, a phoenix of fiery energy emerged through the temples of my soul, calling time on time itself. It was the exact same energy that guides you unassumingly for the very first time to your soulmate before the butterflies of human nature perform their most intense magic to let you both know that you've found each other. The same hypnotic resonance brushed the wings of my heart in reverse to show me lovingly the difference between arrival and departure. There was no difference. The physicality of pain was transformed into heartache so that I could feel something else. It released my soul to flutter with her flight to reach the same lofty unconditional heights.

Carole was showing me her love at its most vulnerable and in her most divine form. I saw at the precise moment of our joint vulnerability what I had to do within and without. There was no difference. We drifted innocently together on wave after dreamy wave in the bluest, most crystal-clear ocean. As love flapped her wings, she turned my attention to many beautiful things. There was peace and calm and beginnings and an ocean of love. Carole was my sunshine, and I was her rain. For one more day and one more day, love would be the sunshine and the rain that breathed life into my rainbows of horizon and hope.

A gentle breeze of heavenly scents lifted the wings that broke our hearts and made them sing. They sang the softest melody of hearts' delight to melt away all fear and fright. A rare and very beautiful butterfly danced with my soul to the enchanted echo of universal silence and softest maternal lullaby. With dreamy whisper and angelic grace, they beckoned to the girl with stars in her eyes and the loveliest smile on her sleeping face. It was beautiful. It was so beautiful it took my breath away.

The only noise was silence and the echo of a child's tears. I sensed in our eternal moment that love had taken flight, but not to leave. This was part of Carole's unspoken wish. She was reminding me, with beautifully broken hearts, that she would never say goodbye. She was giving me a gift of shared memory and had tagged it with an exquisite collection of sense and sensitivity that would never ever seizure. Maybe this was our intuitive resonance, our hearts' desire of the wisdom and alchemy of love. Maybe this was something else, our sixth sense – who knows? I was whispering her name over and over in my head. There was a ringing sound.

I had no idea how long I'd stood at the foot of the stairs. It felt like forever – a thousand years, many lifetimes, maybe longer. My phone was ringing. It was a few seconds, maybe minutes, before the noise registered in my ear. It was a few more seconds before my ear sent the wake-up call to my brain. The hands of time beckoned to me from the wall clock in the kitchen, visible through the open door leading from the hall. I walked slowly into the kitchen and held the phone in my hand. I just stared at it until it stopped ringing. Within a few seconds, it started ringing again. Although I didn't recognise the number, I knew who it was before I answered it.

There were loud medical alarms ringing. I could hear the movement of equipment and people rushing past the caller in close proximity. There were raised voices, the issuance of instructions, and the organisation of something very important. There was urgency. The caller identified herself as a doctor on Carole's ward. She spoke softly, clearly and with purpose. She asked for me by name. I confirmed who I was, and then I listened as she said, 'We are in an emergency situation with your wife, Carole. Can you please make your way to the hospital as soon as possible? Can you do this now?'

I was silent for a few seconds.

She said, 'Do you understand? We are in an emergency situation with Carole.'

I couldn't think. Everything was kafuffled. I just said, 'Yes, understood, on my way.'

She closed the call with the words, 'As soon as you can. Drive carefully, safe journey.'

I just sat on the stairs in the hall and stared at Carole's picture. She stared back at me with a sparkly smile of hazel eyes. I find it difficult to describe what I really felt as love ripped me apart. Carole's world, as I knew it, as I loved it, was evaporating right there and then in a hospital room and right in front of me on the stairs.

All I could do was think about Carole. Brave Carole, inspirational Carole – the right to my left, my love and my lovelier. My best friend, my soulmate, and a wonderful mother stared destiny in the eye, and this time she didn't blink. I was deeply moved, but not because I felt sorry for myself – I never have and I never will – but because Carole had fought so hard with everything at her core to stay for the children and for me for as long as she could.

I have no idea why, but my thoughts turned to Billy. I hoped that during Carole's final curtain call, she would reach out to Billy. Although Carole never really talked about the deepest innermost sadness she endured through and beyond the loss of her unborn child, this was something that she thought about many times a day every day for the rest of her life. I know that she'd made a promise to Billy, and I imagined them together in their ocean of love as she made good her present.

Carole had talked to Billy every day and loved him in her own beautiful way. I had asked her one day how her conversations with Billy came to be.

She just said, matter-of-factly, 'No one is ever lost.'

These are words that comforted me at the times when perhaps I needed them the most.

What to do? I rang Carole's parents. The call lasted just a few seconds. I cleaned my face, changed clothes, and was about to walk down the stairs when my phone rang for the third time. The number flashing on its luminous blue display was the same as the previous two incoming calls – not only did I know the number and the person's voice, but I knew what she would soon imply. It was the same voice as before, but now with much softer tone. She simply asked me if I had left yet for the hospital.

She then said, 'Drive slowly.'

I needed not the words on the end of the phone, but I am forever grateful to have heard them, because they put something into perspective for me. I believe the unexpected but beautiful phenomenon I experienced at the foot of the stairs was of Carole's orchestration. She had composed, quite brilliantly, the symphony of her love, bringing together a percussion of thunder, the stormiest brass, and a woodwind of change. A lonely piccolo delivered notes of dancing sunshine upon which Carole's inner butterfly ascended light of wing, intertwined of heart, and unconditionally of love. I named this musical phenomenon perfected of Carole's nature 'Volo Della Farfalla' in honour of 'the flight of the butterfly'. The lady of my dreams was herself escaping the illusion of life in pursuit of a synchronous world of ideals made manifest by the alchemy of her love.

Carole had known that I would not want her to be alone, that I would want more than anything to be with her. Even in her final hour, Carole had put aside her own needs to nourish and love beyond the boundaries of conventional knowledge and understanding. Perhaps this was a joint effort driven by two souls determined to live together in a moment of eternal presence that is simply the vulnerability and beauty of love. Perhaps this is what's referred to as 'transcendent love'.

Carole had spared me the visual theatre of watching her die in my arms, and yet this was what I had wanted and had conditioned myself to do – not out of duty but forever out of the deepest love. She was again showing me that love knows not condition or boundary, only eternity. I found myself somewhere betwixt the language of love and our love of life. I sat atop the stairs, put down my phone, and wept.

The children were at school. They were safe for a few more precious hours where their lives were almost normal – whatever 'normal' means. They were secure in their own uncomplicated knowledge for just a little while longer. It dawned on me in that moment that my children would never see their Mummy again. My heart broke into a million pieces; each piece bled a million crimson tears, each tear an icy dagger. I needed to be with my English rose at the hospital.

The air was crisp and the sun was shining, but as much as I love sunshine, I took no joy in it that day. As I navigated the empty corridor to the ward, my stomach was in my mouth, my head pounded, and I was shaking. We had always known this moment would come. We always knew there was nothing we could do but accept it for what it was. This was our bond, our love for each other and of each other. My greatest test awaited me. Acceptance was not the test. Understanding was not the test, nor was it confirmation. It was love.

I slowly entered the ward. My shoes squeaked their rubber soles on the clean floor, announcing me. I stood on my own at the reception desk, observing an industry of care and medicine at work. I waited for a few moments, and no one interrupted his or her duties to talk to me or help me. As I waited patiently, I turned on the spot through 360 degrees, looking for a familiar face, a nurse or a doctor or a surgeon. Still no one came to rescue me.

As I rotated, my field of vision fell upon Carole's bed. It was empty. I think I went into shock; my legs turned to jelly. I threw my hands in the air and then cupped my face as love embraced my fragility. I asked for someone to help me. I was invisible, a hologram strobing in and out of everyone's consciousness like a faulty fluorescent strip light.

I don't know how long I had been at the desk when a soft voice behind me whispered, 'Adrian.'

It was the indigo nurse. She took my hand and smiled with shiny eyes, said nothing, and guided me to a side room. I sat down. She pulled up a chair and sat directly opposite me. She was silent and gently retook my right hand with her left and then stroked the top of my hand gently with her right. My left hand supported my head at its outer temple. She didn't have to say anything, and she didn't until I broke the silence.

Looking down at the mottled white tiles, observing the splashing of tears forming a small puddle on the floor, I simply said, 'She's gone, hasn't she?'

The indigo nurse, in softest voice, simply replied, 'Yes. She's gone.'

We sat there together, the indigo nurse and I, as she held my hand a little tighter than before. The puddle on the floor was the only thing in focus. The view from the reception desk of Carole's empty bed came back to me. Her bed had been prepared neatly for the next occupant, adorned with new sheets with square corners and freshly plumped pillows. A shaft of brilliant yellowy white sunlight had landed on the pillows, and dust danced through its ascendant shaft of transparency.

I was screaming Carole's name in my head. I was wishing again that I could swap places with her. I would give my life without hesitation to give Carole back everything she courageously fought so hard to keep, all that she loved and cherished so warmly. She didn't deserve this. Carole never deserved this, but then no one ever does. Perhaps it is neither right nor wrong but simply is.

I needed to be with Carole one last time. Not to say goodbye, because we never needed to say goodbye, and we knew in a strange way that we never really would be parted other than physically. As my head and my heart were telling me to go to Carole, the indigo nurse whispered, 'Would you like to go to Carole now?'

I could only manage a nasal two-word reply: 'Yes please.'

We walked together out of the side room. It was the same side room I had sat in the previous day with Mr White and his team. We journeyed a few paces across the corridor to a private room where Carole was at peaceful rest. The indigo nurse opened the door for me. My heart sank immediately and unimaginably to a depth I knew not existed.

I turned to the indigo nurse and said thank you. She waited with me a short while. I guessed she was making sure I was OK before leaving Carole and I alone together.

The air was calm, still, and silent. The sun was shining outside, and I was raining. My fairy-tale princess, my English rose, looked more beautiful than I could ever remember. My lovely wife, eyes closed, a sleeping beauty. No more pain. Her mouth was slightly open, and a single silver thread of saliva connected her upper and lower teeth at an odd angle. After a moment of being completely mesmerised, I cupped her face so softly with both hands, slowly kissed her smooth freckly skin above her eyes, and whispered, 'I love you.'

I turned to the indigo nurse, who was a blurred silhouette in the doorway, and nodded. There were no words. She departed swiftly with silent feet. The silence in the room was only broken occasionally by the muffled sniff of a weeping man.

I moved to the other side of Carole, to her left side, and held her left hand with mine. After just a few seconds, the most unexpected thing happened. It was so unexpected that it took my breath away in silent gasp. As I held Carole's hand, there was a transfer of energy that passed from her body to me. I can only describe this as being a single intense pulse-like sensation that connected us in a beautiful moment of never-ending heartbeat. The wave of energy tingled through my fingertips before it raced up my left arm, only to disappear at light speed into my chest. It was another gift of the purest kind, and my inner universe sang in awe and wonder through the medium of tears. I felt the grace of Carole's peaceful transfer. Never have I been so moved. Never have I felt love so beautifully.

I held Carole's hand a while longer, never wanting to let it go. We shared a very private conversation. My rose had released the beauty of her love from within and so beautifully without.

When I'd arrived at Carole's bedside just a few minutes earlier, Carole was lying in perfect symmetry. Her soft feminine hands were exposed from beneath the carefully crafted folds of blue woven blanket that kept her warm. Her hands were at rest in a flat palms-down position on the soft cotton bedding. When I eventually summoned enough courage to let her hand go, I placed it gently back into perfect symmetry, just as I had found it. I removed Carole's wedding ring tenderly, kissed it, and placed it in my inside jacket pocket for safekeeping.

In the next instant of time, I looked back at Carole's symmetry and noticed that something had changed. I did a sort of double-take before I saw what it was. Something was different about the shape and contour of both of Carole's hands. They'd still found perfect symmetry but were no longer flat palms-down.

All her life, Carole had slept with her hands in a loose clenched state. By this, I mean she would curl up her fingers so their tips lay gently across the centre of each palm, and the top of her thumbs would be curled slightly inward and bent toward the middle of her closed forefingers. Our children share this lovely phenomenon.

Carole's hands had now found this loose clenched state – perhaps to symbolise a final message of eternal sleep.

This was the second most moving experience of my life. To me, these events were the personification of love and gifted in a beautiful and meaningful way that caressed all my senses with visual, physical, and emotional dexterity. I dropped to my knees, overwhelmed, and wept on Carole's shoulder for the last time.

Not cognisant of time, I heard Carole's voice in my heart as my thoughts meandered this way and that down an endless river of certainty. She said softly just two words and repeated them twice: 'the children'.

Carole's parents had arrived on the ward, and I sensed that it was my job to be Carole's messenger. We cried together before they left to take private moments alone with their little girl. During those intervening minutes, I spoke to the neurology surgeon who was present with his team during the emergency that had released Carole that morning. Dr Blue explained that the increase in pressure inside Carole's head was too much for her to withstand. He went on to say that he and Mr White had spoken on the phone during the emergency to talk about resuscitation. Their professional collaboration was based on many different things, all so clinically important and very real, and had merged into thoughts not to resuscitate. Carole's quality of life, her prognosis, and our wishes had been understood and respected with courage and compassion.

Dr Blue confirmed that he had made the final decision that morning to let Carole flutter by. He apologised for my loss and asked if I had any questions. I had none that he could answer. I took the opportunity to shake his hand and thank him and his team for their professional care and consideration.

I journeyed the few steps back across the corridor to my sleeping beauty. Carole's Mum had very carefully removed the silver crucifix and chain from around Carole's slender neck and transferred it to my possession. I attended to Carole, cupped her face softly with both hands, kissed her forehead, and whispered, 'I love you.' I then did another of the most difficult things I have ever had to do. I had to leave my wonderful, courageous, spirited, and inspirational wife for the last time. I had promises to keep. I could stay no longer. I had sense to take my leave but refused to take leave of my senses.

I'd never thought of that moment before and had never consciously planned for it. I will never find the appropriate quality or semblance of language to describe it, either. I did what my instincts and my fragmented heart guided me to do. I did what Carole would have done. I began the most difficult journey to two brave children. I asked Carole to keep me strong, to guide me, to keep our children strong and safe, and to never stop loving us. I let her know that all of us would never stop loving her. Even though Carole knew this was the substance of our unspoken and unbroken soulmate bond, I found comfort in releasing these thoughts for her once-upon-our-time and our love-ever-after.

I found Dr Blue and the indigo nurse and thanked them for the last time before departing with squeaky feet. Walking down the ward corridor was surreal. I saw my reflection in the glass panel of the door as I approached the ward exit. I recognised the face of the stranger I'd met many times on our beautiful journey through challenge, illness, and the big blue beyond. He too looked different now.

The stranger in the mirror was someone with whom I had become well acquainted. He had helped me to understand myself, Carole, and our reality. He had become my other conscience and the person who listened to reason even when no reason could be found. He was my demon, my salvation, my other new nemesis, and, profoundly, always a friend. He'd never judged me, and we'd never argued. He'd aged that morning. He was lost and was as broken as broken could be. He was someone else now. He reminded me that no one is ever lost. As we exited the hospital ward together, I realised that he was no longer a stranger. He was me.

I walked the loneliest walk through the hospital with Carole's Mum and Dad. I carried a large holdall containing Carole's clothes and her personal belongings. It weighed heavy on my shoulder. It was the same brown leather bag we'd purchased sixteen years ago for the sole purpose of carrying Carole's maternity paraphernalia during her visit to hospital for the marathon birth of our first child. It had been our travelling companion as Carole bore our daughter into our beautiful world. In a reversal of life's hypnotic poetry, the bag was fulfilling the same purpose as a beautiful mother was taken from our world. She too was returning home. It was our bag for all seasons and all journeys, from maternity to eternity. I treasure this bag for all it ever held of emotion, memory, and love in moments forever.

I observed the waiting room where Carole and I would sit holding hands together, sometimes for hours at a time, waiting for her MRI results. This was where we chatted behind our silent fear with positive anxiety of appointment outcomes. This was the place where Carole commanded the inner piano of her soul to play the music of composure, control, compassion, and love – the love that brushed my heart and released my inner butterfly.

I walked past the café where we would buy lunch together and the two pieces of fondant-iced chocolate marble cake we'd take home for the children. I walked past the spot where we would call Carole's parents and send texts to close friends relaying the good news of unchanged MRI scans before we made our way home to our world where we lived to fight another day. With each foot forward, I was thinking about finding ways to continue the fight for both of us. It would be a fight that would test, be painful and cruel. It was the fight to live and to carry on loving. I had piggy eyes, and my inner-mascara was running. I was running to Carole's little butterflies.

I had so many promises to keep and a world to rebuild – perhaps not rebuild but maintain. Two children were unaware of the emptiness that was heading their way forcefully, with all kinds of uncertainty in its wake. There is no amount of preparation that can be undertaken to cope with the loss of life, especially the life and love of a gentle Mummy. I wondered if Carole and I had done the right things when all was said and done, and when some things were undone, unspoken but equally understood. My vision of Carole's empty hospital bed prepared with its square corners for the next patient – was this just a metaphor of reality that simply said life goes on through the nightmares and the dreams that came true? The last words whispered from Carole's lips embodied courage and love.

I was going to have to tell our children that Mummy had gone to heaven. The children didn't deserve this but then no child ever does. There was no anger; there never was. This was another one of those lovely lessons that Carole and I had taught each other without realising it would become a very natural and relaxed part of life. This would become one of the parts of life that I would rely on to navigate new pathways time and time again.

I drove slowly into the road where we lived, noticing that nothing had changed but that everything was different. My senses were amplified in a way that added a super-conscious layer of beauty to everything around me. I'm not sure if it was the contrasting colours of the trees saturated in the purity of sunshine illuminating the magic of nature's transparency, or perhaps the crystal clarity of birdsong that resonated with the symphony in my heart. Maybe it was the whispered breeze of scented wishes kissing the skyline of rooftop eaves and chimney stacks jutting into the bluest and most tranquil ocean sky. Carole was in the sky now, floating on wave after dreamy wave, wrapped in the blanket of her own feathery nature. The sun was still shining on my rose of red and brightest bloom.

I parked the car on our gravel driveway and switched off the engine. I stared again at the man in the rear-view mirror and looked into his puffy eyes. I searched his soul for inspiration, and then I found her. She guided me through a set of rational thought processes which gave substance to a sequence of steps that would get me through the next few hours. It had started. The next chapter was upon us, and it was time to turn the page.

I was in no fit state to collect the children from school and knew that I'd break down as soon as I saw them. Part of turning the page was about balance, stability, and continuity. It sounds odd, doesn't it – continuity? At a time in life where nothing could be more impossible or beyond farthest reach? And yet, these were some of the keys I had to find. I wanted to run, to keep on running and never look back. I wanted to keep the children's school environment a place of safety, without any unkind associations, in the same way that Carole and I had worked hard together to make this so during illness. A little continuity at school would, I hoped, be a blessing. I decided to make this my first priority and so turned a leaf into the fade of an orange and gold autumn – the autumn of my life.

I called upon a friend in a moment of need. I needed help and found it with open arms, a bucket of tears, and a hug of beautiful friendship. Beverly and I chatted for a few minutes, although words were quite unnecessary and in moments impossible. The children would be collected by a familiar face. I phoned school, and everything that we needed was put in place.

My next hour before the children arrived home was incredibly difficult. I sat on the end of the bed in the bedroom Carole I had shared. I stared at her clothes hanging in the wardrobe, knowing that they would never again be animated by her presence. Looking around the room, I found her favourite sweater neatly folded next to a pile of her favourite fleecy pyjama sets. Her shoes and slippers waited patiently for the girl with rhythm and soul who loved life and danced, skipped, and hopscotched betwixt her places in it.

The photo featuring two best friends stared back at me from its home of eighteen years on Carole's bedside table. I reached into my pocket and retrieved Carole's wedding ring and silver cross and chain – two treasures of memory and moment. I closed my eyes and curled up in a foetal position on the bed. Reaching for my Carole-scented pillows, I released my emotions without condition and surrendered. Sunshine cascaded through the open bedroom window and fell once more upon two pillows lonely of freckled face and void of love's own whisper.

The next hour passed quickly. I recognised the sound of a car as it arrived routinely in the street below. I dried my eyes and raced downstairs. The sound of doors opening and closing greeted me as the children arrived and a friend departed. I hadn't thought about what to say or even how to say it, but I knew that whatever was about to happen, the outcome would be the same. I opened the front door to two very smiley children who were probably wondering why they'd been lucky enough to get part of the afternoon off school.

I let fate determine the next three minutes. I smiled as best I could to keep it together just long enough to embrace the amour of a lovely lady upon whitest horse. We exchanged waves, I closed the front door, and so we three retreated to the sanctuary of our four walls, our universe, our home. The children dumped their school bags in the hall next to the bookcase.

As I stood at the bottom of the stairs, I found myself in exactly the same place I'd occupied earlier that day. It was the place where love had marked the spot and joined up some dots. I beckoned the children to me with a frantic circular double-arm movement and began to just sob quietly. Their faces changed as they hugged me simultaneously, one on either side. I circled each of them with an arm and pulled them tightly to my core, their faces buried in my rib cage.

In quietest croaky voice, I just said, 'I'm so sorry, children.'

And I told them. I held them both and kissed them twice on the top of their heads. We stood at the bottom of the stairs and cried together as a family. My heart bled for Carole and her babies. To this day, my grief for them does not stop, nor will it ever. This is my choice to be, to feel, and to see. I wanted to wave a magic wand and make everything go away.

Carole's words echoed in my head: 'You will know what to do' and 'You will be OK.'

It wasn't long before the children sought the sanctuary of their own rooms and pillows.

The bottom stair was again my seat of solitude, and yet within my solitude I am never really alone. Symbolically, this seat is perhaps the place I always find in moments of innermost need. From this place, I've observed the strength, texture, and weave of the fabric of our life many times through the mirror of Carole's eyes. This was a rich and colourful tapestry crafted with love and friendship to withstand the stretching and flexing of fibres beyond all adversity. The fabric of our family was doing what Carole and I had designed it to do. It held us all together in love's embrace through the most important and most difficult times.

Carole and I had done our jobs. Carole did her job, and most beautifully of all, her love has continued to spark a lightness of thought within me to love me through the days when love is the only matter. I sensed that the invisible threads that defined and held together the magical bonds between Carole and her children were still intact, albeit a little frayed at the edges. It could have been much worse.

I love the philosophy that love is itself an invisible thread that is never broken and can never be worn out as long as it's held within. Maybe the 'fabric of life' is another beautiful metaphor that jumps off the page when we need it the most to remind us that the strength of love for each other reflects that which we weave into the fabric of ourselves. I cried in the knowledge that our children could have no greater teacher, and that she'd woven them both into the fabric of her heart. I smiled through a flood of tears in the realisation that the children were Carole's mirror through which love was both teacher and lesson. I am forever the pupil of three beautiful people who show me every day the gift of love. And for this, Carole, I will always love you without condition and so very deeply from within.

9

Heaven Scent

Throughout our family life, Carole and I would often crash with the children in the lounge overnight. Duvets and pillows were strewn everywhere, the sofas disassembled with complete abandonment of structure and tidiness. We would delight in trashing the place for a few wonderful hours. To all of us, this was just a mini-adventure which broke up the routine of normal life. It gave us and the children an opportunity to be silly. We'd eat rubbish all night and watch kids' TV and all our favourite DVDs. We'd play card games and board games like they were going out of fashion, and we always had a blast.

Carole would keep these evenings a surprise for the children and tell them of our plans at the last possible moment. To see the excited expression on their faces when she told them was simply priceless – it was a dream! Carole would plan the evening throughout the day and send me out with a long list of the children's favourite foods for tea: ice-cream, cakes, juices, sweets, and chocolate to keep us going throughout our board-game and TV marathon.

I was never sure who had the most fun, Carole or me or the children. We'd watch our babies fall asleep mid-game under coffee table, in a cardboard box, or just curled in a ball holding playing cards or food and drink. It was lovely. We'd carefully remove any items still under grasp as the children surrendered to the sleep dragon. We'd pop them comfortably into their makeshift sofa beds and cover them up snugly in their fluffy dressing gowns and duvets. Carole and I would watch our children sleep in complete awe of the little stars of our own creation. We'd congratulate each other regularly for our little wonders and marvel at the gift of little lives.

Carole always did what, I guess, a good Mummy does and made sure she could see her children breathing uniformly before she allowed herself to snuggle up to me and go to sleep. I adored Carole's natural motherly instincts, which were fine-tuned in all things. I'd always wait for Carole to nod off first, and then I'd do what we had done together a few hours earlier: I would watch her sleep for a while. I was always mesmerised by the flawless expression of contentment upon Carole's face as she slept. She loved her sleep. To watch her sleep, at peaceful rest after a busy day, stirred my emotions in a way that let me know how fortunate I was to hold her in my arms.

Sometimes, when I had so much stuff whizzing round in my head that sleep was impossible, I'd perfect a neat trick that never failed to summon my own sleepy dragon. I never told Carole about this, but I'd delicately snuggle up so that her minty breath just brushed the side of my face. As I closed my eyes, I'd copy her breathing pattern, and as she melted into the deepest sleep then so would I. I think this was just one of many lovely things that defined us.

The children and I had somehow managed to get through the trauma of the day that Mummy had flown. We were exhausted and struggled with all things emotional and material. I'd spent the majority of the afternoon sitting on bedroom floors in comfort and support of two of the bravest people I will ever know. As the events of the day began to subside, the knocks at the door dissipated into the darkness of a cold starry autumn night of lightly rolling clouds. The phone stopped ringing at about ten thirty. Social media and text messages ceased temporarily for a few hours.

As we closed the door on the last visitor, so we closed the door on a wonderful chapter of family life. The realisation that we would never see, hug, or comfort Mummy again was just so tough to believe, let alone accept. Carole was the centre of our universe, and she was gone. Mummy was gone and never coming back.

I tried to do the thing I always did and put myself in other people's shoes. I wanted to see what the world might look like from their perspective, because from where I stood it looked pretty scary. I contemplated wearing my children's shoes before realising that it was difficult enough to wear my own that day. I figured I'd have to learn to understand my son and daughter as people now and not necessarily as just my children. Our lives were on the accelerated path which was propelling us so quickly into a future of years lost and experience gained. I'd have to find the language I'd used the previous week – fashioned by Carole – when I had to tell them that Mummy was so sick that she wasn't going to make it.

I was scared. *Scared* is probably understating how I really felt. I had sole responsibility for two little lives. Even though Carole had been migrating elements of her parental role to me over the last year of her life, it wasn't quite the same to know that this migration had reached a natural conclusion. By this, I guess I mean that whether I was ready or not to be a sole parent, there was no time for any further training. Did this mean that my training was complete, that I was ready?

I let the 'everything happens for a reason' blanket of life wrap itself around me and acknowledged the curve upon which my learning was really about to start. Perhaps it wasn't necessarily that my learning was about to start, but more about the application of what I had already learned. I had no sense of being alone, and yet I was missing. I was whole, but there was a hole in my heart. It was dark, but I could see everything. Love was still love, but it was different. Perhaps it was more powerful, poetic, and philosophical – even alchemical.

I was still scared. I was scared and frightened to say or do the wrong thing. I struggled with the deepness and intoxication of my own emotions, which tore so violently at the fabric of me that it hurt to breathe. Life hurt, and love hurt even more. The two most important people in our lives would look to me for guidance, strength, support, friendship, and love. They were our world as we were theirs, and as I am theirs so they are mine. I was still missing. I was their Dad and now their pseudo-Mum. But Carole was irreplaceable. I could never be Carole. I'd have to be part-Carole to maintain a degree of balance and continuity on a day-to-day basis.

This is what she'd been teaching me. What would Carole do? She'd pick herself up, dust down, and get back on her bike regardless of how bumpy or muddy the lane. I thought of Carole and the children. I couldn't think of anyone else. I remembered that very sad but inspirational moment in hospital in August 2009 after Carole was told that she was terminally ill. That was one of the defining moments of Carole's life, as her acceptance of her own mortality bore witness to the unfolding of metaphorical wings. I can't control my emotions whenever I think of that day.

I found myself dreaming of memories past in the hall at home on the spot that I now call my bridge. Carole had silently prepared us for a day of moments. She'd taught us with a gentle, subliminal, and almost casual perception that no matter what we go through each day, there is only one thing that is never guaranteed: time. She showed us how important it was that we recognise the value of time, how we should respect the time we have to spend together, and that time is sometimes the only thing that matters. It was time to breathe and to talk irrespective of how much it hurt to do this. It was time to befriend ourselves and each other, and it was time to just be. It was time to be compassionate within as without.

Carole taught me that as time was never guaranteed, so it was constant. It was constant because even when a personal clock stopped at journey's end, time simply carried on, preserving memory to history and holding present tomorrow's gift today. Time is the moment of all moments when we are one with love to realise and to release.

The greatest lesson from my wonderful teacher was that time is also a healer and so, by definition, we would all heal in time. Carole made the time throughout our marriage, and especially throughout her illness, to quietly teach me so many things, and now it was time for me to apply her teaching. This was our day of reckoning and our time to reflect upon a wonderful life. It was time for me to absorb myself in her words of wisdom. Her words drifted with me through my universal silence on a timeless voyage into solitude and inflection. This was the beginning of another lifetime that in time I would understand.

I was daydreaming as I stood on an arched bridge of wooden slats connecting opposing shores of a narrow river. I dreamed that Carole was standing next to me and that we were talking for a just few seconds. I was asking her, 'How can I understand? Help me. What do I do?' She smiled at me with her eyes and almost instantly we were joined for a beautiful moment by a voice, the voice of a child. It was as if the child could hear my silent question and was offering, in a near real-time shift, the guidance I needed. It was like there'd been a fusion of thoughts in which the continuity of reality had somehow bridged my dreamscape. I had been asking a question of Carole through thought when the child answered me. The same child's voice brought my world sharply back to focus as the child repeated a previous answer from the lounge.

'Dad, we're all sleeping in here tonight,' the voice said.

When I think back to that moment, I can't help but cry. As you've probably gathered by now, I cry quite a lot. Tears are my friend. I cried then because it was a moment captured in my imagination which manifested a response in my plane of physical reality. Perhaps it was but a beautifully timed coincidence that served no other purpose than to warm a broken heart. I thanked someone as the bridge below me inverted to colourfully join up more of life's little dots under which three butterflies found sanctuary and flight.

The sofas were disassembled, duvets and pillows scattered. In just a few minutes, the lounge was trashed and transformed into our place of sleep for the next two weeks. As you can probably imagine, sleep was impossible for all of us. I no longer had the sanctuary given by my wife's deep and familiar breathing pattern to comfort me to peaceful slumber. The children and I sat on the sofa. On either side of me they were snuggled into my chest with my arms separately wrapping each of them tightly. We'd been here before, although under very different circumstances.

We cried a lot that evening. We talked a lot too. We remembered all the happy things about Mummy, her wonderful life and our wonderful lives together. There was calm and peace and grief, tears, runny noses, and questions. There were some questions without answers. There was an empty space, a lost voice, her smile and the missing heartbeat of her goodnight kiss. As our hearts and dreams lay broken in a million pieces, we were united by our bond of love for Mummy and consoled by the blanket of reason even though it felt like no reason could ever be found.

Perhaps there is only ever one reason for everything when the layers of life are released to reveal what lies hidden at its very core. Sitting on the sofa with the kids, I knew that in my world, the only reason for life was the lesson Carole had given of herself. She was my inspiration, my courage, and my example for finding footing on firmer ground and going forward one day at a time. Carole was my reason. She was love.

I answered as many questions as I could with a delicate and sensitive edge, trying to put so much into perspective for the children, knowing that it would be impossible to explain everything. I did my best. That's all I could do, all I would ever do. The theme of my replies during the early hours of that Wednesday morning focused on just a few simple things:

- Accepting that Mummy had flown, and understanding that everything, no matter how beautiful, perfect, or imperfect, lasts forever. Everything happens for a reason, and sometimes it's not clear what those reasons are for a long time or maybe ever.

- Taking the wonderful example set by Mummy that sometimes you just have to get on with life no matter how hard things are and make the most of every second of every day. I explained that Mummy and I, with them, had done this every day as a family, and now we had to carry on doing this because that's what Mummy would want us to do. She would want us to be brave just like she'd been, and she wouldn't want us to be sad. I tried to explain that we had been so lucky to have Mummy stay in our lives for as long as she could, and that she had tried so hard to stay as long as her strength and courage would allow.

- Appreciating the friendship and love in our lives. I described Mummy as a kind and loving person. She was the kind of person who taught us to respect the people we care about, the people we call our friends; to value the meaning of friendship; and to understand what this means to ourselves and each other. Friendship was one of the foundations that defined Mummy and made her who she was. Her friendship was so strong that it meant she could love her friends and they could love her every day. They still loved each other even on the really difficult days when sometimes she couldn't always talk to her friends or be there for them because other things got in the way.

True friendship understands that everyone is different; we all have our own lives, priorities, and problems. Just because we don't see people every day or talk to our friends every day doesn't mean we are no longer friends. Some people stay in our hearts even though they may not be ready or able to stay in our lives. True friends would understand this about us too.

Just because Mummy had gone to heaven didn't mean that we were no longer friends. Mummy was a lifelong friend who had given us a lifelong gift – the gift of love. Her love was the most powerful and painful kind. It was a timeless and never-ending love that would make us cry, be sad, and be happy, and it would always be part of us through all the good, the bad, the happy, and the sad.

I told them that even though Mummy had died, her love was something that would never die because in my world of ideals, love lasts forever and a day. Everything hurt so very much because of the love we had for Mummy and the love she had for us. The reason it hurt was because our love for each other was so very strong and so amazing. It was the strongest and most amazing there could ever be.

Through our tide of tears, the three of us decided that we wanted to celebrate Mummy's life with all our friends, with the children's friends, with my friends, and with Mummy's friends. At two thirty, in the wee small hours of Wednesday morning, still snuggled on the sofa with soggy faces, piggy eyes, and so much fatigue, we came up with the idea of something we called Cookies and Candles.

I wanted to take the stigma out of death and everything ugly and difficult it represented, especially for the children and their peers. Cookies were perfect because Mummy was a tough cookie. Everyone loved cookies, and this would be a focus for the children. They could bake them with love and be occupied by cooking and not by anything else other than the special significance that their cookies were to remember Mummy with. Candles were perfect, because they represented a theme for both adults and children in terms of divine light and love everlasting. By tying the two things together, we could celebrate on many levels without fear or regret and remember Mummy, her friendship, her love for us, and her love of life.

Cookies and Candles the celebration was born in a moment of terrible sadness and tragedy, which was somehow overshadowed by a warmer and lovelier optimism. Carole loved chocolate-chip cookies and the smell of warm scented candles, and as if by magic all of this began to make scents of the things that Mummy liked. It felt right. A strange but satisfying moment on the sofa for Carole's three amigos brought interim closure to our day and made our impossible sleep possible for a few precious hours.

I let the children fall asleep and watched in lonely wonder as eyelids closed tight at the end of their most difficult day. I now checked and double-checked and then triple-checked the uniformity of my children's breathing before I allowed myself to rest. I closed my eyes and remembered Carole's face as she used to sleep, tracing her soft features and her closed eyes in my mind.

I had a flashback to the last morning in hospital with Carole as she lay peacefully in her symmetry. The top of my nose tingled on the inside, and I screwed up my face in pain as my eyes shed in torrent. I held my head in my hands and flipped back to a vision of her resting in sleep, lying next to me and breathing heavenly as she used to. This time, her face, although beautiful and peaceful, was different. She was crying in my arms, the arms that longed to hold her just one more time until the end of time. I was crying with her. Her breathing got deeper and deeper, as did mine. Carole was in eternal sleep. I repeated softly the last words I whispered in Carole's ear and kissed her lips in my dream.

After an hour or so, I drifted into a heavier sleep than usual, not heavy as in deep uninterruptable sleep but deep as in thought. I had dreams about Carole, the majority of which were unclear and confused. In Carole-speak, my dreams were *kafuffled* – slightly out of the ordinary, not real but with a sense of odd reality about them. Carole used this word often to describe her recovery sensations immediately after seizure. I dreamed that Carole was standing over me with bright shiny eyes, wearing her favourite grey-and-black-striped jumper and a pair of deep blue skinny jeans. Her smile was always a thing of beauty, but at that moment it was at its most bright.

She whispered to me in her soft ethereal voice, 'Bun? Are you OK, Bun? Are you OK?'

My sleep was abruptly broken, and I woke with a start to find Carole standing over me. As quick as she was there, she was gone. My heart was racing, I was sweating, and if I'm completely honest, I was terrified – I didn't know if I was dreaming or if this was real. It felt real. I wanted it to be real. I was crying real tears. I wondered if this was just my imagination and pondered the notion that imagination and reality are both very real and that maybe one cannot exist without the other.

Over the next few weeks, I would learn that some of Carole's friends had experienced similar visits to their dreams. It was as if Carole was checking up on a few of her loved ones with one final act of care and farewell to tell us in her own way that she was OK. I regret not understanding that moment with her until much longer afterwards, although now it is one of my most treasured memories and remains as vivid as it was then.

I couldn't get back to sleep. It was just so odd not to have to think about the journey to the hospital, about schedules, logistics, school, lunches, and the medical milestones that drove us through a short-term future. All I could think about was today. We just had to get through today, remember how we did that, learn, adapt, and then do the same thing tomorrow, the same thing the day after and the day after that. Oh, and smile. That's what Carole did.

I had work to do. The children would be awake soon, and reality would hit hard. They would be tired and irritable and probably hungry. Breakfast was the first order. Over breakfast, we recapped the Cookies and Candles conversation and, still in agreement, decided to plough on and get organised. Eating our way through croissants and fruit juice, we determined that Saturday, 19 November 2011, would be the day our Cookies and Candles celebration would take place. Just three days were available to organise.

We made a list of the things we needed to do, and throughout the day we managed to get them all done. Ingredients for chocolate-chip cookies were purchased; white wine, red wine, beer, and soft drinks of every description were bought and stockpiled in the garage. We bought candles, matches, and candleholders. Invitations were created, printed, and delivered to all the neighbours. We sent out e-mails and created an event on social media.

The three of us worked like a well-oiled machine over the next three strangest of days. We were communicating; we were listening and sharing and doing something that would have made Carole smile. We were doing remarkable stuff with focus, inner strength, and just a little hint of fun that provided a short-term distraction from our very weird reality. We were doing this for Mummy. We were doing it together, for all of us.

Each evening preceding our special celebration, we ventured outside into the cold night air and lit the train of candles in all shapes, sizes, and colours we'd placed around the front path of the house. The children had helped me move the picnic table from the back garden to the front. This was where we sat for an hour or so each night just watching the candles dance in the breeze as they cast a kaleidoscope of shadows and colours onto the house and into the crisp night air. There was a really special sense of magic each evening as the glow lit up our world temporarily to replace the sunshine we had lost.

Our neighbours would venture out from time to time to chat and offer their own candles, and we'd reminisce about Carole. A wonderful scene created through tragedy and grief helped us to look at loss with a less heavy heart for a few hours. Sometimes dressed in pyjamas and dressing gowns, we'd blow out the candles before we went to bed. We'd found this a sort of therapy, I guess, and an unusual but effective way to relax before sleep as we talked about candles and Mummy. I found a small glass of my favourite red wine was a fine accompaniment. In lovely association, we were learning to talk openly about the last few cruel weeks by reference to some of the things we were doing to celebrate Mummy. I hoped in my heart that she could find a way to share in these lovely moments. Maybe she did. My heart tells me so.

We crashed in and trashed the lounge only to reassemble it every morning. We grieved together with honesty and openness, which began to galvanise our bond of friendship a little more each day. We enjoyed the relative security of each other and our own four walls, our home – a home built with love by Carole. For me, a sensitive and deeply emotional chap at the best of times, it felt like these moments were beginning to define the people we would become on our never-ending journey through time. These moments set a strong emotional foundation upon which we would find the strength and courage to reinforce all the beautiful parts of life built and protected for us by a special person.

I couldn't be more proud of my children, who were doing what their Mummy always did so well. They were giving adversity a huge kick where it hurts and being fearless. Whether they were aware of this was irrelevant. It was both lovely and heart-breaking to witness. We had such a long way to go. This was the best start I could have ever hoped for. My children were already learning, adapting, and growing. They have their Mummy's courage.

Saturday arrived. During that day, the children spent hours in the kitchen making dozens of cookies. They made white-chocolate ones, some with plain chocolate, and even experimental offerings with marshmallow and raspberries. The kitchen was alive with activity and some humour. Given the significance of this day, it was heart-warming to see. I'd prepped the front garden with lanterns borrowed from neighbours. Our train of candles were replenished, the tables were just about holding up the weight of alcohol placed upon them, and some tea lights lit the way to our cottage of Cookies and Candles.

At around five o'clock, we started to receive a few guests, and the train of candles crept quietly around the side of our lighthouse. The number of carriages grew longer and longer, each filling the air with a plethora of scents and dancing shadows. From the responses we had received on e-mail, text, and social media, we'd guesstimated throughout the day that maybe thirty or forty people would join us to celebrate Carole's life. The children's friends started to arrive, and they bought their Mums and Dads and siblings. Our neighbours bought their children, and our friends bought their friends and relatives. By about half past six, there were over a hundred people in the street, on the front lawn, in the road, on the drive, and in the house. Everyone had brought cookies and candles, and some had brought homemade cakes as well.

It is difficult to put into words the display of friendship, support, love, solidarity and remembrance given so freely by so many. I'd never hugged and been hugged by so many beautiful people. I'd never heard so many people saying so many lovely things. I'd never seen so many cookies in one place! The air was abuzz with lively conversation, as people who all knew Carole but did not necessarily know each other engaged in banter about their mutual friend. All these people, Carole's dear friends, all there at that time for Carole, for each other, for the children, and for me – to be absolutely honest with you, it was just so overwhelming.

There were times when I found things too much to deal with and had to find a quiet spot out of public view to cry happy and sad tears. I did this several times over the next four or five hours. It was never long before someone would come and find me. When I managed to grab a few minutes of quiet contemplation alone in the back garden, I looked to the heavens and wondered if Carole could see the scene before me. I thought about what she would make of it all. Carole would be so humbled, so shocked that so many people were joined in celebration of her love. She would cry too.

Even in flight, Carole had continued to unite so many people for a few short but memorable hours. I can't find words powerful enough to convey the depth of love I felt that evening. In the darkness, I found another little light, maybe many little lights in the eyes of friendship.

At regular intervals as the evening unfolded, I would seek out my children to make sure that they were OK. What was lovely is that they also did the same for me.

One of my abiding memories of that buzzy evening was opening the front door to my house and seeing my daughter surrounded by her closest friends. They sat on the stairs or were huddled on the wooden floor in the hall talking, holding hands, linking arms, and eating cookies. They were together doing what teenage friends do. It was a very special moment for me and very moving to see, inspirational and just lovely. It reflected the bravery and compassion of young people wise beyond their years and without fears. Friendship had found its own way into everyone's hearts that evening, and we all had Carole to thank for that. Each of us in our own way had done exactly that.

We had enough cookies to feed a small army for the next three weeks. Friends came and went throughout the evening, although the number of people at the house seemed constant throughout.

Two of our thoughtful neighbours – they know who they are – had brought some Chinese lanterns with them. The children and I decided that at around ten o'clock, we would light the lanterns in the street. This would be our loving tribute to Mummy. It would be our perfect but simple and deeply meaningful finale to a very special day. We could continue the theme of candles and light eternal by sending our flames of love to the heavens. We had eight lanterns to release altogether. We'd let people know throughout the evening about the finale, and as the time approached a quiet excitement filled the night-time air.

At ten o'clock, the thirty or so friends still celebrating with us assembled up and down the close, and we distributed the lanterns to make preparation for flight. Small groups of three and four formed naturally without any organisation. In no time at all, a smoky haze filled the street and the smell of burning wax fused with the candle scents already filling the air.

The train of candles around the house was at its longest by this time. Each flame flickered with a magical glow expelling a stronger fragrance, deeper shadows, and more intense illumination of the plants and trees in close vicinity. Those who weren't directly shaping, lighting, or holding lanterns were taking photos and offering words of encouragement to the groups now doing all these things.

The first lantern was ready for flight, and my children and I let it go with all our love into the night sky. We watched with tight embrace its silent ascendancy toward the stars. A brilliant sphere of vanilla light animated by the brightest ball of orange flame flew perfectly skyward to the twinkling embrace of forever. Carole's favourite colour was orange, and she was always mesmerized by the flicker of fire and flame.

There was no applause or cheering. The beautiful sound of universal silence echoed across the rooftops and through the trees – the sort of sound that you hear inside an empty place of devotion or a theatre of dreams. Everyone's gaze and attention was diverted to the heavens as one by one the lanterns were released with a little prayer or a paraphrase of love and sentimental whisper. There was a lovely procession of light in the sky as the first and second lanterns floated gently into space, getting smaller and smaller as they ascended. The third and fourth lanterns were released and then the fifth, all following the same flight path equally spaced and each as illuminating and emotionally provoking as the other. The sixth followed in quick succession as the first and second lanterns now faded out of sight, spending their bright orange fuel and completing their symbolic journey from earth.

The seventh lantern was special. Chinese lanterns let you know when they are ready to take off. When the saturation of hot air inside their flimsy outer skin of opaque paper is completed, the lantern tugs its way skyward through your fingers with gentle assurance that the time is now to let go. This was a heartfelt and deeply poetic moment for me. My thoughts were redirected to that wonderful moment in hospital when I held Carole's fingers for the last time. The ethereal moment when she told me lovingly that it was her time to fly lit me up like a Christmas tree on the inside as I stood in the street. The seventh lantern was released to the heavens with love, this time from the tips of my fingers.

The eighth lantern was a different matter. The team of friends managing this one tried and tried and tried again to get it airborne, without success. Flight of the eighth lantern was now impossible, and a little moment of sadness ensued because we had ended a wonderfully emotional evening of success and celebration on a flat note.

My sadness was short-lived, as my children whispered to me, 'Mummy's favourite number was seven!'

Perhaps it was a coincidence, or a lovely acknowledgement from Carole that seven was enough. The hopeless romantic in me believes that life is often touched by just a little magic here and there when we need it most, or sometimes when we just turn our attention to other things. The romantic notion that Carole had maybe tugged at my core to release a sublime moment of magic fused thoughts of our everlasting love.

My heart was aglow with fire and flicker, and I hoped she could see, sense, and feel my love for her. The seventh lantern was ascending uniformly with simple ease, and I watched with an emotional tingle and wet face as it disappeared gently from my watery vision. It is one of the most magical sights I have ever seen. It was simply breath-taking.

One of the most magical evenings of my life, filled with so much from so many for someone just a little bit special, was drawing to a close. The train of candles continued to flicker long into the night, lighting the gravel pathway around our home and bringing it to life. Little yellow lights replaced the darkness of day with a calmer, more peaceful, ethereal incantation with each hypnotic flicker and quiver of heavenly scent.

10

Nature's Way

The children and I would remember our evening of Cookies and Candles with much affection and a positive sadness for a very long time. Our joint family objective had been achieved. We'd managed to make the evening a lovely success with the help of all our friends near and far and never forgotten.

The following morning, there was much work to do. There were pots and pans and baking trays, stacked three and four high, left over from our cookie-making exploits. They covered every inch of every kitchen work surface. Glasses, paper cups, and empty bottles were scattered in the garage, around the house, and in the front garden. Several trips to the bottle bank were needed. The outdoor wooden furniture used to carry the weight of wines, beers, and soft drinks was put away. Anything borrowed from the neighbours was returned. Some of the leftover cookies fuelled us through a relaxed nostalgic endeavour to clean house. By late afternoon, it is safe to say that we were all pretty exhausted and a little jaded.

When darkness fell, as we'd done the previous week, we ventured out again into the stillness of night and relit the train of candles around the house. Under the stars, the three of us sat at the picnic table in the shadows of candlelight and talked about Mummy and our experience of Cookies and Candles. We looked at some of the photographs taken the previous evening and found some very special images. It was an important time for all of us. I'd wanted to make sure that we never felt awkward talking about Mummy or about our memories of her and with her. At the same time, I was aware of the importance of balance and treading gently one step at a time, one foot in front of the other, one day at a time.

My emotions were scattered, loose, and often ungrounded in those early weeks. If I'm honest, one step at a time was all I could manage. Our little evening ritual of lighting candles and nibbling through the remaining cookies over the coming days and weeks provided a vehicle for us to journey from one moment to the next and then from one day to the day after. I hoped that we'd find these evenings comforting and safe so that talking and sharing with each other remained part of our own natures.

In a beautifully difficult way, I was beginning to realise that we were able to continue to travel together without condition because Carole had promised herself that she'd never hide anything from her children. I could simply follow her lead. I let the children know that if there were some evenings that they didn't want to light candles or were too tired or simply found themselves doing something else, it was OK. That said, we found ourselves outside in nature most evenings over the next four weeks as we took some baby steps together, one at a time.

* * *

Cookies and Candles was an emotional high point of those days after Carole's death, but there were also occasions when I'd have to attend to the administrative and emotionally difficult aspects of losing the one you love. There were protocols to observe, arrangements to make, letters to write, e-mails to send, telephone calls to make – so many telephone calls. Journeys were started and decisions were reached.

On Thursday, 17 November 2011, two days after Carole's death and two before our night of Cookies and Candles, I travelled to the hospital in London for the last time. I'd remembered to buy petrol the day before. I was alone in the car with only my thoughts, memories, and melancholy for company. This was my first time travelling to the hospital without nervous anticipation of outcomes. There was no need to scan my emotions to seek the root cause of tranquillity and tears. It was very weird. I'd switched the radio off so that I could think clearly about all things past and present without interruption.

My interactions with Carole two days before as she took flight from her carousel weighed heavily. There was a sense of beauty, reassurance, and sadness as my vision of Carole lying in perfect symmetry brought the rain and a smile. I felt stuck in a world that was alien – a world that didn't feel right without her. My world would never feel right without Carole. It was a world where I would scream silently every day when, just for a few minutes, I would relive partial seizure of memories intact and smile through the pain.

For the past two days, I'd been looking for some other signs that Carole was OK. This was something on my mind, and even now, when I think back to our first ethereal moment together, I can't really explain what I was looking for. All I knew, maybe just sensed, was that there were still some missing pieces to the landscape we had started to paint together. There were still a few things that made no sense, and I had a very strong sense of unfinished business and incompleteness. Trying to figure this stuff out in the car was impossible. Just as I'd decided it was time to herd those thoughts and questions to their own place of rest, something happened.

Traffic had ground to an abrupt halt as I joined a stationary queue on the motorway. Even though I had an appointment to keep, time had become just a transformational concept in my life. It had taken on a different meaning and another dimension. I'd usually worry about being late, but not that day. That day, I was travelling to formally register Carole's death. Time had no power over me. I had all the time in the world, and time was no longer my master.

I needed music. I decided it was time for music. Heart FM, Carole's favourite radio station, was still auto-tuned, and I caught the last few lyrics of a song as I switched on the car's radio. It was not a song I recognised, nor did I know the identity of the beautiful voice who brought to life the most poetic and poignant lyrics. Whoever it was had the voice of an angel as she moved me to an ocean of tears. She rescued me at precisely a moment of need. I repeated the lyrics over and over in my head so I'd remember them. By the time I arrived at the hospital about forty-five minutes later, I could only remember 'wherever you will go'. I wrote these words down on a piece of paper and then promptly forgot about them.

I had travelled to hospital that day with a head full of thoughts racing in every direction. They had collided with each other, and my head hurt during the journey home. My heart ached because of the heaviness of the task I had completed. I'd registered the placement of a diamond in the sky. Now I could begin to organise Carole's final journey to her place of earthly rest, her place in nature. As this process began, there were so many decisions to make and lots of things to think about. The events of the day so far had overwhelmed me.

I went home and shared a headache of solitude and heartache with my new friend in the mirror. We talked openly about the best way to approach the things that needed to be done over the next few weeks. We conversed again through the reflective surface in the bathroom. After much deliberation, the two of us agreed that I had to involve the children in the decision-making process. It was another one of those things we had to get through together, and besides, Carole and I had agreed that we would never hide anything from them. I wanted the children to be connected to a difficult but important period of their lives. I also wanted them to know that they had a choice. They'd always had free will, and one of my promises was to assure this with steadfast continuity.

That afternoon, I sat with my two best friends on the sofa in the lounge. The sofa had become a poetic place of safety, comfort, heartfelt communication, and understanding. The three of us talked safely and sensitively about what we all thought we should do. They let me know that they wanted to be part of this process. We chatted about the various elements that we had to bring together and the arrangements that had to be made to celebrate Mummy's life. Between us, we made some important decisions, and we did this with mature thinking, level-headed practicality, and a little humour.

Things started to fall with gentle feather-like motion into place. When I think back to those moments on the sofa that afternoon, a tide of compassion and wonderment lift me gently to a place of bewildered awe. This is the place I will forever keep safe the emotional hearts of my best friends.

Carole had always carried copies of the children's passport photos in her purse. These pictures were taken when the children were one and four years old respectively. At some point during every day of her motherhood, Carole would take these photos out of her purse and trace every contour of her children's faces to memory. It was almost as if she knew that one day she'd be unable to do that anymore. We wanted Mummy to take something personal with her and decided that these photos were our perfect gift, as she'd always cherished them. The children also wanted a family photo of the four of us to accompany her at rest. We selected one of our favourites.

We also had to choose the clothes that Mummy would wear. This was a relatively easy decision – PJs, dressing gown, and slippers. I'd bought Carole a very special T-shirt for her birthday that year: it had a picture of her cat on the front with the words 'I heart Tigger.' When she'd opened this present, she'd cried with love for us and in memory of her best feline friend. I remember as she kissed me on her last birthday morning, to say thank you for her presents, her tears dropped silently onto my face and ran down my cheeks and under my chin before tickling my neck. The children and I agreed that Mummy would wear her Tigger T-shirt too. We selected her favourite slippers and a pair of warm bed socks. As Mummy was now in eternal sleep, we figured she'd like to be dressed appropriately, and we wanted her to be warm and snuggly.

We made copies of the photographs, wrote messages on the back, placed them in an envelope addressed to 'Mummy, with love always x x x', and put them in one of her dressing-gown pockets. Her favourite dressing gown was the one made of fluffy white cotton and patterned with soft hearts. I'd washed it, and it had the tranquil fragrance of mystic flowers and lotus blossom.

We had to decide on a date and time for Mummy's funeral. As Mummy loved Christmas, we chose 1 December, the first day of Advent, to join together a few old friends for one last time. It would also mean that every year, this date would have an extra-special meaning in many ways. It would symbolise the advent of a new chapter in all our lives. A Christmas without Carole, without Mummy, without Santa's little helper, was a dire prospect, and one that was never going to feel right. The first question Carole had asked the neuro team during our conversation on the day of diagnosis reverberated in my head.

'Am I going to orphan my kids by Christmas?'

Christmas this year would be a very different one for us. The excitement of Christmas past was, for the time being, a step too far.

On a breezy afternoon the following week, the children and I ventured to the cemetery to search for a place we thought Mummy might like best to sleep. It didn't take very long to find the perfect bed. We chose a lovely spot on the end of a brand-new row that overlooked a very special place dedicated to angel children. The sun would rise and be seen from her new place in nature, and it would blush in the evening skies behind her. This was for me deeply meaningful and another poignant reminder that Carole was always the sunshine in my heart. The thought of sun shining brightly upon her for the majority of each day warmed me, as this is what Carole had given me and the children so lovingly all these years. It felt right.

Over the next few days, we talked again about the order of service and what would be the most appropriate music and song. What would Mummy have wanted? All the time, Carole's words in my head kept me emotionally honest when all I wanted us to do was simply run and fly away with her.

'You will know what to do.'

As we made decision after decision, I began to realise that actually, Carole was right. We knew what we had to do, and we were doing this together as a family. Carole had trusted us unconditionally. Through our trust in her, I think, our hearts were making the right choices and guiding us over the bumps in the road. Love was our invisible map; sunshine was the hand that held the light to show the way, and the stars were our compass. I will always think about her words and the insight she had to prepare us with so few of them. These were wise words that gave warmth, strength, and direction when she knew we would need them the most. In another way, perhaps Carole was saying that whatever you do will always be right. It will be right because you will follow your hearts, and to follow your hearts is to truly find me again. To find me is to know that you never lost me – and no one is ever lost. She was beautifully clever.

Carole's most favourite flower was the white lily, so we agreed that white lilies would adorn her casket. The order of service was assembled. In keeping with the theme of favourite things, the children thought that the music and song should relate in some way to school.

My daughter made the inspirational connection to the end-of-year leaving assembly for Year 6 pupils. This was an annual event at school that Carole always attended, regardless of whether one of our children was in Year 6. She would always sob her way through a very emotional assembly on the last day of the academic year when the school bid farewell to its mature pupils. For these children, the assembly marked the beginning of a milestone journey into a new world of education, experience, and growth. It marked a time of flight for the pupils and the turn of a page to the next chapter of their lives in which they would progressively find their own wings.

Given Mummy's very close association with school and the significance to our own journey, it seemed almost magical to connect a few of these things together. We decided that the music and song from the leaving assembly was a lovely, meaningful, and subtle tribute. I rang the head teacher, outlined our thoughts, and we discussed the possibilities over a cup of coffee in her office. As we sat and talked, a white feather, caught in a cobweb on the outside of the office window, swung gently back and forth in the autumn breeze.

I mentioned this to the head teacher, who remarked, 'Yes, I know – it's been there for a few days.'

It was a lovely moment. The head teacher wanted to organise something very special for us. Her school choir would sing two of Carole's favourite assembly songs. The first was 'Paintbox', also known as 'Cauliflowers Fluffy'. Carole was fluffy. The other song was 'Leaving on a Jet Plane', written by John Denver in 1966. This song was originally called 'Babe, I Hate to Go'.

Over the next week, the school choir's moving rendition of both songs was recorded to CD so that we could hear the choir of little butterflies singing these songs in the chapel during our celebration of Carole's life. When I first heard the lyrics for these songs, I realised how very special this choice had been – inspired by the deepest love. 'Paintbox' was about foods that grow in nature and 'Leaving on a Jet Plane' was about time, departure, and memories to hold.

There was just one big-ticket item left to organise. We had to decide on the venue to get together for a drink with some special friends after our service of celebration. Just around the corner from the cemetery there was a golf club. I thought Carole would be tickled by the idea of us having a few drinks there on her behalf, given her love of Wii golf. This also fitted very nicely into the theme of the day, which was all about Carole's favourite things.

I popped over to the golf club and had a chat with the manager, who had worked there for thirteen years, about our requirements.

He looked at dates, times, the number of people, etc. As luck would have it, the bar was free for a few hours during the afternoon of our special day. Everything had fallen into place.

Well, nearly everything. I was still searching for my very personal connection. In keeping with the theme of connections and Carole's favourite things, I wanted the service itself to have a special significance. I wanted to bring together aspects of my life with Carole in a way that was deeply meaningful to me. I had a few ideas, but none really sat comfortably with my need for a very ordinary, meaningful, and simple celebration of love.

After a few busy days of planning and organising, I sat on the sofa quite late one evening to check and balance all the things that needed to be done. I managed to check off all the major items on my list. When I got to the last item, I found myself staring into space for a few moments. Without realising, I had started to tap the black biro in my right hand against my bottom lip.

I'd already lit a few scented candles and placed them in symmetry on the brick fireplace. The walled light seemed low, and my eyes were tired and puffy. I'd switched the TV off, and my cat, Whispa, who'd quietly snuggled up to me, had fallen asleep curled upside down in a ball of white and cream fluff. As I tapped the pen, I looked around the room.

Without warning, I was emotionally overwhelmed. A very heavy sadness descended out of thin air. It felt like an invisible cloak had been wrapped around me so tightly that it was almost impossible to breathe. My heart quickened, and I felt it sinking. In the next breath, a well of tears overflowed like a bath tap I couldn't turn off. These were my emotions. I was crying, but it was as if I had relinquished complete control.

Everything started to remind me of Carole. I imagined her sitting next to me. She was smiling, a picture of perfect health and happiness and pain-free. Her white piano was idle, but her music echoed silently through scented air. A photo of Carole with the children looked at me from its frame on the brick shelf atop the fireplace. The photo spoke a language of emotion that only my heart could hear and understand. It was the same family photo that the children had chosen for placement in Carole's dressing-gown pocket.

I thought about the five-year milestones we'd jotted down; we'd got just under halfway. Carole was only forty-two, forever young. I was holding my head in my hands and blinking uncontrollably as if about to seizure, just like Carole would've done. My thoughts meandered randomly, trying to make sense of my senses. I was stuck on something to do with Carole's age that made no sense. For a moment, I didn't know where I was, and everything was unfamiliar. I brought my hands to my face to fix the temporary mask of reality. I couldn't stop my heart breaking into a few more pieces.

I closed my eyes and, without warning, found myself in a room I didn't know. It was dark and there were no visual boundaries of perspective or points of reference. A woman who I sensed but couldn't see whispered so softly to me and repeated just one question: 'Do you understand?'

Then I realised something that would kiss my heart again and again for a very long time. It was about Carole's visit to a clairvoyant many years ago. Carole had been told that she wouldn't see her Mum reach the age of 76. When Carole and I had spoken about this before she became ill, it was clear to me she thought that something would affect her Mum. As I sat on the sofa, still in my state of overwhelm, it occurred to me that during her illness, Carole had understood the true significance of the ages. Carole had realised that the message was indirectly about her own mortality.

I had understanding. I had understanding and clarity. I understood that Carole had lived with this knowledge silently and never mentioned it. When she had said to the children that she sort of knew when she would die, she had perhaps intuitively joined up some dots, put two and two together, and connected her future to the past. In the present, I just sobbed.

My gift of understanding that evening was a presence I will cherish lovingly beyond the end of time. Time, I remembered, was no longer my master. My emotional bath tap opened full bore once more. Even though Carole was naturally of strong character, it was difficult to comprehend the inner strength she found to live through each day of the last two and a half years of life knowing what she knew. In 2011, Carole's Mum celebrated her seventy-fifth birthday. Carole moved me during every day of our life together in so many unique and beautiful ways. That evening on the sofa, she moved me again to another realm of understanding, another beautiful moment of love's absolute overwhelm.

After a short time, I was drawn back to the piece of paper on the oak coffee table. I was back in the lounge on the sofa, staring at the final item on the list: 'book golf course'. I searched the room again to make sure I wasn't dreaming. Whispa was still asleep next to me curled upside down. The Wii remote control was visible from the open door of the oak TV cabinet. The brown leather footstool was about five feet away from the TV, where Carole would position it to play golf. One of the candles had gone out, and symmetry had become displaced. I could hardly keep my eyes open and felt very light of head. It was late as a scented mist filled the room. It would have been about the time that Carole and I would play golf. We loved this time of the evening. I let myself play one more round of memory, reflection, and inflection before thinking about sleep.

Wii golf had become a sort of evening ritual at home, and it brought out a usually silent competitive streak in Carole that was a joy to see in action. Carole always positioned herself on the rectangular brown leather footstool. Dressed in PJs, dressing gown, and slippers, typically high on her much stronger evening meds, she'd perch her glasses strategically on the end of her nose and prepare to duel.

Wii remote at the ready, she'd throw down the gauntlet, always with an unintimidating, 'Ready to get your butt kicked, Bun?!' And off we went.

To say this became a ritual is probably an understatement. It was a fiercely obsessive but friendly rivalry, a bit of fun between two soulmates who found their inner children during midnight's playful hours. It was also a test of memory for Carole. It was fascinating to observe her concentration when working out wind speeds, distance, angle of shot, and club selection. Sometimes it would take three or four minutes for her to make these choices, but she'd nearly always execute each shot with jaw-dropping precision.

This fascinated me, because even though my lovely wife spoke a second language, could complete the Rubik's cube in under a minute (sometimes blindfolded), and was a competent chess player, when it came to working manually with numbers she was bamboozled! Any of her school friends could no doubt recount her lack of mathematical prowess. Ask Carole to add together three single-digit numbers and you would see panic, hesitation, and a humorous collapse of logic.

Carole had a mental block with numbers, and yet when I think about some of the things she excelled at, they all involved numbers, number patterns, and number processing in some way. It was painfully ticklish, almost cruel, to watch Carole determinedly push mental dexterity of usual brilliance in an attempt to process what should have been a simple calculation. She would forgive me for saying that we laughed with her during these moments which were perplexing for her but so beautiful for all of us. They were beautiful because Carole would laugh so much, especially when she got the answer wrong, that she'd have tears rolling down cheeks bright and rosy with embarrassment. She laughed so much that we often had to remind her to breathe, as her blush changed very quickly from rose to cherry to deep aubergine.

There were some evenings playing golf when my butt was kicked so hard I'd very childishly try to put her off her game by introducing the concept of numbers to break her concentration. Needless to say, my attempts at very obvious and underhanded misdirection never worked. What I'd soon realised was that Carole didn't ever apply a complicated scientific strategy to playing golf. Well, actually, *I* didn't realise this. The children told me. And Carole told the children knowing that they would tell me. What made the whole thing even funnier was that she knew that I knew, but I never told her that I knew. Bluff and double-bluff always had the last laugh – which was usually on me!

You see, Carole used to beat me at golf because she observed how much the wind blew the flag on the pin. She listened to the sound of the wind instead of reading its speed, and she observed the contours of the green. In her own way, she used nature to guide her. The other stroke of genius she pulled – and I will always, always love this – was insisting that I go first. I thought she was being naturally charming and thoughtful when actually she was simply outsmarting me. She watched what I did, saw my mistake, and corrected it intuitively with her next shot. If I ended up thirteen feet away from the pin on the green, Carole would finish up seven feet away. If I hit a shot into the bunker, she would miss the bunker, and if I over-hit a shot ... well, you get the picture. Personally, I put my defeats – of which there were many – down to the use of performance-enhancing drugs!

Carole's approach to golf was a little like the approach she used to cope with her life during the challenging years. There was never really any room for science in Carole's world. She always looked at everything in an uncomplicated but nevertheless thoughtful and very practical way. This was her sort of 'mind over matter' approach to getting on with things. It helped her with the small matter of keeping a sound mind on the course that her life would force us both to play.

To play golf with Carole every evening was a privilege and a pleasure. Nothing was ever taken too seriously, but it was seriously fun. It was fun because we were each playing with the right partner. In her own way, Carole showed me that life is a lot like golf. It challenges and presents obstacles. No two courses are ever the same, and each person plays the game slightly differently from everyone else. Carole evolved her understanding of the courses she played using a technique that she fashioned based on her needs and her capabilities at that time. Carole dreamed of beating the course record one day, although winning was never really her dream. Her dream come true was simply proving to herself that she could do it.

As Carole's playing partner, I had to improve my own game just to keep up with her in the end, so in a lovely way, Carole was again my teacher. I suppose you could say that we learned from each other. Carole holds the course record at home of twelve under par over nine holes. It is a record that has never been bettered, and one that I am so very, very proud of. I'm not proud of just her record but ever more in awe of the way she played her game. I'd joke about her use of performance enhancers, and we looked forward to our enjoyment of midnight's playful hours on many an evening.

Carole's performance enhancers in life, though, were never really her drugs. Carole surrounded herself with the things that made her life enjoyable, happy, loving, lovely, and lovelier: her children, her friends, her family, her cats, and all of her favourite things. She did the things that she loved to do, and every day her love for the children pulled her through depths unimaginable. I guess you could say that Carole's drug of choice was her love of life itself. Not every day produced a dream round, but to play every day was Carole's dream.

As I alighted my dreamscape, a friend streamed my tears and I wiped his face. Through blurry eyes, we ticked off the final item on my list and smiled. The light had faded as the remaining candles' spent flicker emitted enchanted swirls of haze in release of genies from their lamps. I had one last look around the room before turning off the wall lights.

Plugging in the earphones of my iPod, I headed up the wooden hill. I'd wanted to find something relaxing to listen to before going to sleep. Overtired and emotional, I played the song that had captured my imagination on a journey into the unknown the week before. I'd searched online, found the song, and bought via download Charlene Soraia's beautiful version. Listening to this track on my way upstairs was the perfect way to round off a day of difference and heightened emotional sensitivity.

Ascending the stairs that evening was, I think, the moment I fell in love with the romance of music. 'If music be the food of love, play on,' were Shakespeare's words that would eventually comfort me in my slumber on a twelfth night of solitude. I loved the lyrics of 'Wherever You Will Go' so much that I decided they had to be part of our celebration of love and life. My favourite lyrics would be printed on the back of the order of service.

Whispa followed me up the stairs and jumped languidly onto her usual place of sleep atop Carole's pillow. It wasn't long before my feline companion was fast asleep again in a ball of fluffy, purring perfection. Perhaps if love was a sound, it would be the unconditional vibration of a very happy pussycat. As I closed my eyes to summon the hypnotic haze of my own sleepy dragon, so Lady Synchronicity returned to tap me on the shoulder and kiss my sleeve once more. She was the magical mistress of memory-scape whose cartography marked the spots with love just as love joined up her dots. She was the echo of life singing the same song through every peak and valley of a rich emotional tapestry, pointing to the obviousness of that which we know but choose not to seek. She showed me a platter of lyrical romance splashed with Shakespeare's insightfulness to nourish the continuous motion of love's play on the infinity of our imagination.

'Wherever You Will Go' was written by a band named 'The Calling', whose original track was featured in one of Carole's all-time favourite films. Charlene's version has rescued me many, many times and always at the precise moment of my heart's vulnerability to *Love Actually*. Perhaps this lovely song has been the calling of many more people to be or to see love.

* * *

A few days later, the first day of December 2011 had arrived. It was the first day of our different advent. I awoke to find the room a lot darker than usual. The alarm on my phone sang into life to let me know it was seven a.m. Squinting through eyes half-closed, I casually opened the curtains from the sanctuary of my duvet and pillows. Kneeling on the right-hand side of the bed, I peered out through the open window onto the gravel driveway. It was difficult to see any of the neighbours' houses beyond a grey silhouette of the tree in the front garden just a few yards away. A bank of damp precipitation danced in the cool morning air to the sound of hypnotic birdsong in the distance. It was foggy.

Carole, I recalled, used to say that fog was nature's blanket.

This morning, a dense blanket of fog had lovingly wrapped itself around our house. It incubated and kept us safe for just a little while longer until we had to venture out into our own mist. The previous evening, we'd left one or two of the candles alight outside in their train of carriages below the kitchen and dining-room windows. A vanilla scent wafted heavenly into the bedroom. This reminded me of Carole. We'd left the candles burning quite by accident and had simply forgotten to blow them out upon retiring to sleep in the early hours. Carole used to forget things sometimes too.

Then it dawned on me: For the first time in sixteen years, the children didn't have Advent calendars to open this morning. With all the activities, organisation, and preparation for the celebration – many of them still in progress – I'd simply forgotten about the calendars.

Carole would never have forgotten to do this, I thought.

She may have forgotten many things but never the calendars. I perched my elbows on the windowsill and held my head in my hands, temples icy, consoled only by nature's blanket as it crept in through the open window and gently kissed my face. I was thinking about the day ahead. As the fog began to lift, so I had started to rain.

Even though the past fifteen days had been difficult, the children and I had been focused on getting things ready. We'd survived together one day at a time and then one more day after that. The scent of sweetly fragranced wax and the shimmer of sparse yellow candlelight on the path below reminded me of our evening of

Cookies and Candles. The children had been brave beyond their years that evening. They'd been so brave, not just for the last fifteen days but the past two and a quarter years, and yet their new journey was still in its infancy. Their courage was about to be tested again. I woke them up. Breakfast was first order, and we ate together in the lounge.

Photos of Carole were all over the floor next to my shoes and a tin of black wax polish. My recently dry-cleaned dark grey single-breasted suit was still in its polythene wrap and hung on the back of the glass-panelled lounge door. A new packet-creased long-sleeved white shirt hung on a hanger from the middle of the door frame, waiting to be ironed. Whispa had curled up on scatter cushions on the sofa next to a large transparent box full of family photograph albums. A tatty-looking copy of my twelve-minute speech – decorated with folded corners, circular coffee-mug stains, and last-minute edits – was draped over the left-hand side of the brown leather foot stool. Over croissants and juice, the three of us recapped on what we still had to complete before we were to depart the house at 12:10 p.m.

Milly finished some delicate cropping and positioning of photos of Mummy into an album. We'd purchased a new album to keep safe some special memories and planned to share these with friends later that afternoon at the nineteenth hole. A matching book of condolence, decorated with the same soft velvety cream fabric and a gold mosaic heart, was also made ready.

Alex helped me to practise my speech. He timed it and made some recommendations for improvement as he listened to me over and over again until I was word perfect. I practised as I ironed my white cotton shirt in the dining room. I cut out a paragraph or two and made final edits to finish a few seconds shy of nine minutes. I knew it by heart. A fresh copy was printed, folded, and placed in the inside pocket of my suit jacket along with a personal copy of the order of service and Carole's gold wedding ring. Alex placed his Mum's silver identity bracelet in his jacket pocket, and Milly wore Carole's silver cross necklace. We each had a piece of jewellery about our person as we prepared to return our most precious jewel to nature. A few phone calls were made and received as we finalised all the last-minute preparations. As we got ourselves ready, I repolished my shoes and finished tying a Windsor knot in my favourite silk tie – a gift from Carole.

The stroke of midday arrived. There was time for one last look in the mirror, whereupon I found a friendly face whose compassionate smile and watery eyes needed no words to share his story. I collected a bunch of soft white lilies from the garage, situated adjacent to the house, and then we jumped in the car and began a journey of journeys. The lilies were just beginning to open and reveal their inner beauty.

Everything was just a little surreal as we drove the short distance to Carole's childhood home. In the hallway of her Mum and Dad's house, the children and I decided there and then, without any thought, that we should salute Mummy in a way that would've made her laugh.

We looked at each other and said, 'Janice.'

On the count of three, the three of us knelt on one knee in the style of Atlas holding the world on his shoulders and saluted our own goddess of bowling for the last time. We had a group hug for Mummy, and then the moment was upon us.

Two long black polished limousines pulled up outside in the street and rolled to a silent stop. Language has insufficient words to describe the emotion of that first moment your eyes, heart, and soul register this image. The children and I were escorted to the second limousine with Carole's parents. We drove away very slowly and in silence before I turned to the children with love bursting from my heart and welling up behind my eyes. In a very gentle voice, I managed to squawk a message of love.

'There are sometimes moments in life that define the people we become. As hard as this is going to be, this is one of those moments. All we need to do is get through today for Mummy and for each other, and then we will worry about the rest of our lives tomorrow. I am here for you now.'

As the car drove quietly around the corner, a lady walking on the footpath stopped and bowed her head as we passed. It was a very lovely moment narrated to the children by Carole's parents during the remainder of our very short journey. Looking out of the window of the car, I noticed that the sky was blue. My heart was showing me that my sky is always blue.

As we drove into the grounds of the cemetery, there was a sweeping left-hand curve to negotiate before we reached the entrance to the chapel. As we cleared the part of the curve lined with trees, the chapel appeared in view. Some of our friends had chosen to wait outside to greet all of us, and we drove a little way past them before rolling to a gentle stop. I will never forget that moment or the next forty-four minutes of my life, because it was just too lovely – heart-breaking, but so very lovely.

We waited for only a few minutes while our friends found their seats and then we followed Carole into the chapel. My daughter held my left hand and my son held my right. The echo of universal silence filled the air for a pregnant moment. The music started and then deepest breath. There was no dimming of house lights, although in the world that was our theatre of dreams, we were saying farewell to one of its super-troupers and a very lovely leading lady, the flower of my heart. Roses are red.

The chapel was full of Carole's friends and loved ones. Every seat was taken, and those who could not find seats stood lining every inch of wall. As the music stopped, we found our seats, and so our celebration of love began. In just a few minutes, I would be reading my speech. As I sat between my children, everything was a blur, a little fuzzy, and I wanted to scream. I wanted my carousel to stop and for my own flying horse to take me home. I couldn't see a thing and nothing registered through my ears but the sound of a distant bell whispering on the breeze.

The only thought resonating within my racing heart was, 'This isn't right – I must be dreaming.'

I heard my name, and it was a few seconds before my ears sent the message to my brain. It was time to read to my rose. I arrived at the lectern just a few feet away and with, very shaky hands, placed the neatly folded pages of my speech in front of me. I looked very quickly with the heaviest of hearts at my two best friends, who were now seated together – a moment I will remember always. No words. I had no idea how I would get through the next nine minutes. There was a sea of colour and faces and there was love, so much love. As the universal echo of silence returned, so it was filled with the whisper of dreams.

I placed my hands on either side of the lectern and unexpectedly found the energy to make sense of my senses. It started with a glowing sensation in the innermost sanctum of my heart. It radiated through my arms, hands, legs, feet, and head. Almost instantly, I became aware of the lightest touch of tingly sensation that fell through my whole body from head to toes. It was like being tapped with a magic wand that sprinkled dust to animate a myriad of beautiful feelings. In the blink of an eye, my nerves condensed into butterflies, which fluttered for the shortest moment in my stomach before evaporating almost as quickly as they'd transformed me.

I found myself saying, 'Thank you.'

I had found my own very private connection. I was thanking Carole. I wanted to cry. The next nine minutes of my world were beautiful. They were beautifully tough but beautiful all the same, as the backdrop of universal silence amplified once more its eternal whisper of love's echo. The next few lines are some of my favourite echoes.

I cannot let this moment pass without mentioning Carole's feet! Most of you have probably never seen Carole's feet – and there is good reason for this. Carole would be horrified for me to tell you that they were size eight – so I won't do that! Her feet were to become part of a memory game we used to play during her final stay in hospital so that she knew she was talking to me. Carole struggled with memory loss quite a bit due to the location of her glioma. She would say to me, 'But how do I know I am talking to you?' and I would say, 'Well, ask me a question about your feet.' So she would ask me the same question to demonstrate that she remembered: that question was, 'Do you love my feet?' And I would always give the same response: 'No, I hate them.' She would always reply, 'Now I know I'm talking to you,' and then she would smile a thousand smiles!

In all seriousness, Carole's feet are symbolic of her journey through life. Her feet were the foundation upon which she stood tall and the carousel which carried her through childhood, through her youth, to me, into married life, parenthood, and through her final challenges. She was a colossus to so many, striding with depth and strength into long-lasting friendships – friendships she valued, upon which indelible footprints were left within the hearts of so many. I will always adore Carole, especially her feet – and remember them with much fondness, saluting the path she walked without fear or complaint.

The love we have for Carole knows no boundaries and is not constrained by time. We know that Carole's love is unconditional and that she could not love us more than she does, and she knows the same of all of us. While our hearts and dreams lie broken and in a million pieces, we are united by our bond of love and consoled by the rationale that everything happens for a reason. As we rebuild our lives together, that reason for me will always be Carole. She will never abandon us and will be forever our inspiration to carry on one day at a time. We will try to follow her selfless, brilliant, and yet ordinary example. God bless my darling and sleep tight with the knowledge that we will always love you. Farewell my lovely. Always three kisses: x x x.

I faltered on the last few words. There were to be no goodbyes, only the fondest of farewells. Our celebration continued as 160 friends all sang along with the school's choir of little butterflies remembering our own Cauliflower Fluffy and the plane from which she had departed. The acoustics of love announced chapter's end at our own assembly of leaving and of flight. I found harmony with the waterfall of life as we dropped naturally into a rocky abyss of splashing foam and muffled underwater bubbles.

One of Carole's best friends forever read a small but perfectly formed passage from a well-known book, referencing 1 Corinthians 13. This text is simple, for it speaks of love. These words move me every time I go back and absorb myself in them. The service was beautiful, and it finished almost as quickly as it had started.

A train of friends and family snaked a mournfully quiet path out of the chapel under a foggy blanket through which there peeked a sunshine haze and blue sky. Short of distance and long of carriage, we travelled together in the company of courage, celebration, and love to her final place of rest in nature. The children and I surrendered the white lilies to the earth as we replanted the seed of our hearts.

I often wonder if Carole had had the choice to clear her own path, whether autumn would have been the backdrop to her final postcard. Maybe this was her choice of love, actually. My heart tells me every day that it was. 'Leaves in Autumn' has a much deeper significance these days, as does my rose of a beautiful summer.

To the many friends who lovingly accompanied Carole and her family throughout a beautiful life and to journey's never-end, I simply want to share words that should only be felt, not spoken. 'Thank you' seems wholly understated, though I send this unconditionally with endless love on a rainbow of senses for all your seasons wherever you will go. If my rose be red and your sky so blue, there is infinitely but one beautiful place between I and you.

11

Messages

It was just a few days after Carole and I had started our separate journeys. The children and I were in the process of talking through our celebration plans for Mummy's funeral. Preparations for the evening of Cookies and Candles were in full flight. The paperwork that needed filling out had been started, although there were times when I really didn't know what to do or even where to start. There was a hole in my heart and a whole in my life.

I'd received a lovely offer of support from Carole's best friend of over thirty years to help with all the forms and formalities. Angela had offered to sit with me for a whole day while one document after another was completed, stuffed in an envelope, and stamped ready for dispatch. It was a lovely gesture that remains always in heart. I am so grateful because it reinforced quite quickly that I wasn't ready to fill out any more forms and, rightly or wrongly, I didn't want anyone else to do this for me. It just didn't feel right, so I decided to wait until it did. It would take me over two years to put the final administrative elements of Carole's estate to rest.

On this particular afternoon, I sat at home in the quietness of the dining room with laptop open and a very large glass of my favourite red wine. There were photograph albums on the table and on the floor and some beautiful black-and-white photos on canvass hanging on the wall. It was calm. I was calm. My thoughts drifted this way and that in their avoidance of both arrival and departure. Every time I closed my eyes, I could see Carole's face or hear her voice. I had a sensitivity of memory which made all that appeared of imagination feel like it was real. I knew it was real because it hurt so much.

I watched several video clips of Carole, who was beautifully and quintessentially animated as she played in the winter snow with the children and as we shared a humorous, relaxed, and very watery theme-park ride one summer's afternoon. There were so many photographs and moving images of the four of us having the most amazing times. An album of our wedding photographs lay open on the wooden farmhouse-style table on which I rested my elbows. The album showed two photographs of my fairy-tale princess in her wedding dress getting out of the vintage navy-blue wedding car in the rain.

As I stared adoringly at these pictures, drifting back to the magic of the day, I noticed what looked like a single white feather stuck to the roof of the car. It was in both photographs, and yet I'd never noticed it before. Its discovery was a moment of inner loveliness that bought warmth and a smile.

Browsing the photos and my moving landscapes of memory, it was surreal to think that the mother of my children had whispered the most beautiful and selfless farewell. It was mind-numbing to know this. To feel this made not much sense of anything. My inner child couldn't help but sob quietly through memories and moments – all of which were happy and of purpose. I sobbed at the realisation that our todays had become our yesterdays and there were no more family tomorrows. All of our yesterdays were the most special days because they were now our memories. I think that was the first moment I'd acknowledged, or allowed myself to acknowledge, the never-ending depth of emotion that is a broken heart.

Carole's white piano stood idle in the lounge, missing its entertainer of moonlight's fantasy sonata. Her picture on the bookcase in the hall smiled once more to welcome us home after another busy day. Her shoes lined the lower shelf in the shoe cupboard under the stairs next to a row of three or four handbags whose contents were untouched. Carole's clothes hung in the wardrobe, her cosmetics were neatly positioned in the bathroom cabinet, and her handwriting filled the dry-wipe notice board covering an alcove wall in the kitchen. The scent of her favourite perfume hung unmistakeably in the air whenever I cried. The fragrance of her kiss and the lightness of her touch made of scents the flower called love-in-idleness.

With every breath there was emptiness, and within emptiness there lived pain. Wherever I looked, whatever I listened to, and wherever I went, there was no escaping the symphony of Carole's unique signature. Walking to the shops, seeing couples holding hands, or driving past a mother pushing a pram in the rain – these and many more catalysts of memory all bought forth a cranial brochure of imagery and emotion. It was with me wherever I will go. It was lovely. It was beautiful. It cut deep so much sometimes that it was difficult to breathe. I guess it always will be–– and that's OK, because this is my choice, it's what I choose to be, to feel, and to see. The emptiness is a kind of void that nestles into the shoulder of my psyche to remind me how much I loved and was loved.

Sitting alone in memory lane, I became unexpectedly overwhelmed by a question that flew to me quite out of the blue. It was something that I hadn't thought about at all, and it caught me a little off guard. What was I to do with Carole's stuff? Carole had stuff everywhere – this was her home, why wouldn't she? I had no idea what I was supposed to do. I sat for a moment or two in this really weird place of familiarity and oddity. What were my options? Did I just take everything away so there would be no visual connection to her? Or did I leave things exactly as they were? What about the kids?

Sitting in the moment, it dawned on me that what I was actually beginning to feel was no more or less complicated than I wanted it to be. It was difficult to know where to start or what to do, just from a self-preservation perspective. I started to play through one scenario after another and then another, and I got nowhere fast. So I applied the same thought processes that Carole and I had always shared in the face of our day-to-day quandaries. We'd talk and just work stuff out in a way that slotted into the balance of our life.

I relaxed my mind. I arrived quickly at a silent but sensible state of mental composure and decided to sit for a little while and see where my thoughts would take me. In the overall scheme of things, what I did or did not do with Carole's stuff really wasn't any more important than what was for dinner that evening. Then I realised that this was, after all, a simple matter of choices. I'd made a decision about all the paperwork and chosen the path that best suited me in my moment. I could do this about Carole's stuff too – about anything. I was learning to trust my innermost feelings, and this was a completely new and different experience in itself.

I decided to take another leaf out of Carole's book. I gave myself permission to feel – to feel unconditionally. I wanted to feel the intensity of my innermost heartache, sensing intuitively that I had to descend into the bowels of my emotions to truly understand the paradox that is 'love hurts'. This was only ever about honesty, true emotional honesty of self. Selfishly, I had always centred my life and responsibilities on the needs of Carole and the children. I loved doing this, as they fuelled my life with abundance and love. Whether I liked it or not, it was time for me to take stock of my new life and evaluate how best to structure and organise it. I had to find a way to maintain the balance that Carole and I had previously worked so naturally to find. This was always going to be one of my most emotionally adverse challenges.

During the time of Carole's greatest adversity, there were moments when she had to let go of her natural need or desire to support me in pursuit of her own needs. Whether Carole liked or disliked these choices was to a great extent irrelevant. As she sought her own inner guidance and inner balance to meet her personal needs, so she trusted me to understand and remould the distribution of our collectiveness. We still managed to do things together for each other and our family, and when the need arose, there were things that I would do instead of Carole and vice versa.

We'd sometimes have to experiment with the frequency, combinations, and dosage of different drugs to create optimum relief from seizure, so Carole's energy levels would fluctuate. When this happened in the afternoons, she'd sometimes transfer to me the responsibility for cooking our evening meal. The children and I would understand that this was simply because Mummy needed to sleep. We were able to do these things quite effectively, almost seamlessly, because we invested the time to talk honestly to ourselves and to each other – and we always did this with love, without second-guessing the outcomes. There was a natural safety in whatever the outcomes were and an unspoken trust, maybe an emotional bond, which told us we were going to be OK anyway.

I could sit there on my own and feel sorry for myself if I wanted to or, in Carole-speak, I could do something less boring instead. No one would blame me for curling up in a ball and hiding away from the world for a while – that would be a choice I could allow myself to make. We're all different at the end of the day, and to some people curling up for a while would a great thing to do, as would stopping the world for personal or collective moments of feeling and healing. What I did or did not do was my choice and mine alone. It was mine alone, and being alone was my challenge. It was mine to make and no one else's to judge. I had to do what was right for me and then think about what was right for me and the children.

This is what Carole and I had always tried to do, and together we'd simply created the best opportunities for the success that we defined based on our needs. Everything was different without Carole, but it changed not that which my heart continued to know, to teach, and to be taught. If anything, Carole had amplified that which I always held lovingly at the heart of my world. I decided to follow my heart and be guided by its ever deepening ache, and so let myself drift upon the rivers it cried every morning and every evening, with each candle, and always when I closed my eyes.

There is a school of thought that says change, no matter how big or small, can always be managed. How I chose to do this was up to me as an individual. Perhaps my unique brand of self-management is based simply on the way I looked at things – the way I see things through my own eyes and maybe the hearts of others. Sometimes I will openly admit that I don't like change, but if I stop for just a second to think about change, I find it in everything everywhere. It is ever constant, whether I like it or not. I'm now aware that I manage some degree of change all the time – what to wear, what to cook, how to love and be loved, when to be strong, silent, or supportive of self and others. Change is everywhere, and we are each our own makers and managers of decision.

Perhaps love is my perception. I find myself these days looking at life and love from a different perspective or a different angle. I do this not because I have to but because I want to and because I can. I want to learn. I see things differently in terms of problem and solution or question and answer. This is what makes change manageable for me.

I've always viewed emotional change, on the other hand, as a very different beast. It requires a delicate and more refined transparent lightness of touch which embraces the sensitivities of self before other. It isn't necessarily always just about what I see but perhaps more about what I feel when I combine my senses together. If I encounter something that stirs the echo of emotions, the lesson was always mine to interpret and translate what had stimulated thought and how that made me feel and behave.

If I saw Carole in pain or in seizure, the lesson for me was how do I help, support, and love her. If seeing Carole in seizure made me angry or unhappy, the lesson was still the same – how could I help, support, and love her. When I saw this repeatedly, the lesson was always the same. If it changed, it was only ever how to help her more, support her more, or love her more, without forgetting my own compassion for self.

Looking at all the photographs, I sensed a need to surrender again to the darkest depths of my emotions to explore more of love's honesty. Even though it hurt like nothing I'd ever felt before, my heart was guiding me gently to this place of uncharted understanding and clarity. I closed my eyes and dared to dream. Of distant gaze, I dared to go to see her face of sunshine glow, to walk, to talk, and to understand, but mostly just to hold her hand.

What I'd started to do was let go, although I hadn't properly understood this as a well-rounded conscious process. It would take almost three years of my life to truly appreciate how very beautiful love is and has always been. I say this most carefully, because loving Carole and being loved by Carole has been the most uniquely beautiful experience of my life. It has taken me three years to understand that love never dies. Within the context of my life and love of Carole, this is truly the enchantment and beauty of my gift of her love in our moment forever. My rose is red and her moon so blue of once-upon-a-times and dreams come true.

What to do about all of Carole's stuff about the place? I grabbed a cup of coffee and did this thing I now call sitting in the question. I closed my eyes and focused my thoughts, repeating in my mind a question. I guess it was the same process I'd adopted all those years ago in the bowling alley when I described Carole's wedding dress to her. I concentrated on my breathing for a moment and then imagined a single intake of breath moving through my torso, with vapour-like swirls finding the chambers of my heart, like a genie returning to its lamp. I imagined the question in words surrounding me through 360 degrees of symmetry. I drifted to a visual canvass looking down upon myself as I sat crossed-legged in the middle of words and worlds.

As I sat, eyes still closed, I relaxed my breathing and thought about some of the things that might help me to solve the puzzle. I thought about what Carole might do. If we sat and talked on the sofa, what would she say and how would I read her emotionally? Had we gone through a similar metaphorical dilemma together? Could I draw positively from the outcomes of those experiences?

I had one of our sofa conversations in my head. Exploring our abstract nature, I mapped an image behind my eyes of some of Carole's possessions occupying their respective places around the house. As I did this, I noticed possessions floating mid-air above their places of relative belonging. It was Carole's stuff that took to hovering. The house was much older and the furniture was antique. There was a grandfather clock and an ornate hourglass of platinum sand which just didn't fit with anything. After a few seconds, everything drifted gently feather-like back to its original residence. What was this showing me?

I sat a little while longer. The answer began to emerge through a process of thought which was both obvious and yet profound. It was obvious because – well, it just was. It was profound because I felt and then trusted the emotion of the answer, thus knowing it to be the right one. It was the right one for me in my moment of need and present. The answer was to leave everything gently in its original place – perhaps for another passage of suspended animation which we commonly referred to as time. It was snowing in my heart.

As I sat with my laptop open for another hour or so, I continued to receive messages of love and condolence. I'd posted online an album of photographs the day before which had invoked some very lovely feedback and sentimental whispers that hugged my soul. Occasionally, Carole and I had sent each other silly and sentimental messages on social media just to say 'I love you.' As I browsed through the many recently received messages, I opened our message history and looked at the last few Carole and I had exchanged.

On 7 November 2010, I'd sent Carole a message to say, 'I love you.'

On 15 November 2010, Carole had replied, saying, 'Love you more.'

What I hadn't realised immediately was that these two particular dates were of poetic and profound coincidence exactly one year later. The last day that Carole was at home before she started her final stay in hospital was 7 November 2011. The date that Carole's flight took us in different directions was 15 November 2011. I wonder sometimes if there is more to life than meets the eye, held in heart for moments of love. Perhaps life is but a journey of beautiful coincidence for our enjoyment and appreciation of love in a moment forever.

* * *

Carole's children, family, and friends were always held close in Carole's heart, wrapped in a blanket of love's finest weave and autumn warmth. For an hour every day during her working week, Carole had wrapped the same blanket of her loving nature around the children she looked after at school. All the schoolchildren knew her name, and Mrs Jones knew all of their names too – although she did get a few of them mixed up sometimes!

At home, we'd been managing change for just over two years and had been able to do this with a compassion and sensitivity for each other that found progressive strength, day by day. What I'd not understood properly, or given time of understanding to, was that a community of children who were friends with each other and Mrs Jones were facing a journey of sadness and heartbreak of their own. Carole's work colleagues were managing emotional change within an environment of the most delicate care and compassion, not only for Carole but for all the children and each other.

Just a few days after Mrs Jones had released her wings, I received, at home the most amazing and very beautiful handmade card from Year 5 pupils. I am looking at it as I write these words, and it is so beautiful that it helps me to cry happy tears. My best friend told me one day that 'tears wash all the heartache away.'

On the front in very colourful letters, it reads, 'Mrs Jones and Family and *Friends*' and there are feathers stuck on it – two are pink, one is blue, and one is green. There are four feathers, one for each of us and colour-coded so beautifully. There is also a handmade paper flower, a pink rose. Six pieces of paper have been folded in half and glued on to form flaps which open. The front of these has the loveliest hand-drawn pictures of Mrs Jones and opens up to reveal heartfelt messages from the children and the teachers inside. Some of the messages read 'Thank you for being so caring and thoughtful,' 'Thank you for being a wonderful lunch time controller you always looked out for us,' and 'She has been a lovely person, very *preaty, considerit*, and very, very funny.'

On the inside of this thoughtfully beautiful card there are red and purple hearts and flowers and rainbows and more messages from the children. There's a cat and a dog and some smiley faces. One of the children wrote 'PS – see you on the way up.' And finally, on the back of the card is a paper pocket and inside the paper pocket is another piece of paper. All of Year 5 had written their names on this and drawn more hearts, stars, and lots of kisses. This card has a very special place of its own at home and in my heart. It is a poignant reminder of the innocence and beauty of life as seen through the eyes and hearts of children who shared in an eternal moment the sensitivity of their own natures.

Two weeks later, on 13 December 2011, another gift from school was presented to my family. The value of this gift cannot be measured, for it is priceless. It is a book 'in loving memory' simply entitled *Mrs Jones*. It has no less than 106 beautifully handwritten messages that tug at the heartstrings of life, releasing the music of love to fly from every letter and word on each page. It has the wonderful presence of moments to treasure that echo friendships of sense and sensitivity from pupils and teachers alike. Each message is as beautiful, thoughtful, and thought-provoking as the others.

There is one message that jumps off the second page and hugs me every time I open my book in loving memory. It reads, 'I *rember* when I got lost and she found me.' Bless. Lady Synchronicity really does get everywhere, doesn't she? School was one of very few places outside the security of our home where Mrs Jones could be herself.

I extend a message of the deepest heartfelt thanks to all the children and their teachers with lovely wishes from all of us forever and always with lots of love and three kisses x x x.

12.

Of Love

When I look back on my family's experience of living with challenge and living through opportunity, I am surprised and overwhelmed by the emotional distance we've all travelled together. As individuals, the four of us have coped with things unthinkable and unimaginable. Once this starts, I realise it never really stops. It becomes acutely less painful over time to live with difference as long as we treat each other and ourselves all of the time with honesty, compassion, and kindness.

Our differences are the fears and uncertainties of the horrible and unknowing kind. Many thousands, maybe millions of us traverse this same heartbreak every day. At some point in our lives, we all have to do this. It's one of those things that we do, yet perhaps it's the most difficult and most intensely felt of all things. It can be part of our human nature and our psyche to make things unnecessarily difficult for ourselves and sometimes for each other in moments of struggle – but it doesn't have to be that way. Emotional honesty and communication are the keys to finding a less bumpy inner path.

Above the surface of this journey I continue to call my life, I found there to be no end to human kindness. In the face of those things which take fragile life and turn the tenderness of love into the art of memory, there is always kindness. It is a kindness which is born and given only of love, with love, and for love. I watched, sometimes helplessly but with so much love, how Carole challenged herself to be the devoted other to me and a devoted mother to our children. Below her surface, she found opportunity to turn all the negative things caused by illness into positive outcomes by pushing to one side her own needs to focus on those of others. In doing so, she pushed aside her fears and surrendered to herself through kindness and inner giving. Was this the paradox of 'love hurts'?

As she did this for us, so we did this for her, and a natural almost subliminal balance was restored. I see this now as a sense of unspoken beauty and a very powerful love. At the time, we just found ways to cope together and for each other. Carole switched her thought processes and so changed what she saw and how she processed visual and sensory transactions, which transformed how she behaved. Carole found through acceptance a way to balance mind and body, to become peacefully at ease with the disease at the heart of her life. She was our mirror, as we are of her.

What is inspirational for me, looking back, is that I understand she swam against the tide of physical illness, of emotional and mental fatigue, and did this with the grace of a swan and always with a smile. Carole showed me that despite her heartbreak, she found life and her love of it to be of more value than anything else. She let us see how determinedly she grasped the opportunity to live for one more day and for as many more beautiful days after that, just as her nature intended. When I say *live*, I really mean living her life to the fullest, regardless of the things in her way. She laughed in the face of adversity and smiled through her pain to grasp an unbridled passion and love for life which was never idle.

As she did these things, she never lost self-control, self-compassion, or her compassion for others. She learned intuitively to be kind to herself. Carole never felt guilt about being ill; she never complained and never used terminal illness as an excuse not to do anything. It was as if she forgave herself for having to leave us all so soon, and so she attracted the same deepest compassion and love from those she loved.

As I continue to reflect upon our collective travels, my knowledge of Carole grows by the hour as the true depth of her love never stops revealing its beauty beyond anything I could previously touch or dream. Love, Carole's love, has opened my eyes in ways unthinkable and unimaginable. It challenged me to write this book in the face of my own grief, to create an opportunity for the release of everything I hold dear in my heart. It has been difficult at times to know what to do or what to say. It's been a lonely path of my own choosing, as I've taken time to get to know myself beyond the duality and illusion of my mirror of life. It has forced me to find, to know, to embrace, and to love all that is above and below and within and without my emotional honesty.

There have been some days, and I'm sure that there will be many more too, when the philosophy of life made no sense. On one of those days I just stopped – I stopped everything. I stopped being. Nothing made sense, and the harder I tried to understand, the more nonsense I found. I'd had a wonderfully insightful moment of loveliest vulnerability, of fizzy water and lime in the midday sunshine, but it made no sense so I decided to stop looking and started listening to the health of my own heart. Once more, I stopped *being*. I started to *begin* and so *began* to write about a wonderful girl who never stopped loving.

As I immersed myself in the depths of honesty, I found a love that intensified with each metaphor of sharpest incision that cut through the denial of my own self-expression. I searched my soul for inspiration, as I've done countless times, and looked love and grief straight in the eye. Wherever I went, I could hear, see, and feel love in ascendancy over all other things. I knew then that love was and is the lesson of all lessons. It is my lesson. It had always been my lesson. It will always be my lesson.

I thought about how love runs through the veins of our lives, creating challenge and opportunity, and how both of these characters yearned to create more love. I thought about how love defined Carole and how love was never a challenge for her but more a statement of intent to be, to feel, and to see. I realised that to live a dream, it must be held of happiness and in heart and given freely of love and with love and maybe for love. Carole and I lived out our dreams and found the happiness we both sought for each other and our children. Our happily-ever-after had manifested itself through the surrender of our deepest fears, our truest thoughts and the heartfelt emotions we held for each other and together as one.

Carole always said to me that she'd live anywhere, under a bridge or in a cardboard box, as long as we were all together. Never in a million years did we ever expect not to grow old together, and yet we managed our lives through very difficult times, accepting it was always supposed to be. Perhaps this was love acting and reacting in its purest form, as every action has an equal and opposite attraction. Perhaps love is simply the purest form of energy balancing the inner and outer universe of our collective consciousness – the ether we sometimes share of dream, thought, and creative expansion.

I had so many questions, but the one question I never asked was *why*. The only questions of any importance were always *how* and *when*. The answer was always found in love – just like in fairy tales and all the dreams that come true.

Once upon a time, I found love wherever I looked or wherever I wanted to look. It was hiding in the stars of my midsummer's night sky, between the lines of an unwritten book, in a stolen kiss of idleness, in the softest hand I long to hold, and in the confectionary of love's hearts. It was the light in everyone's eyes and behind every smile, but how I saw this, I realised, was of my own choosing. Sometimes love found me when I least expected her, and even when I turned my attention to other things, she flapped her wings and whispered the loveliest things. Even in grief, I found love to be as powerful, as beautiful, and as invigorating as ever before. Perhaps this was because I let it be these things. I absorbed myself of it even though it hurt so much. Perhaps this was because I trusted my love for Carole and so trusted love as she was and is intended to be.

I found love in language and in my use of language, which became much more measured, thoughtful, forgiving, compassionate, and kind. Words like *evolve* and *revolve* hid the contextual supposition in silent suspension until I was ready to see it clearly without condition but within my heart. Maybe I didn't see it because I had no need to feel it's intensity until our own natures decided it was time to expand our knowledge of love upward yet another notch of sensitivity and flight. If I think about love in the context of an evolving emotion, perhaps Carole's love is my never-ending gift of evolution. Perhaps the real gift is the mindfulness of presence and the brush of butterfly kisses upon my heart. In personal terms, maybe I have to know myself inwardly to love all that is good, bad, and indifferent – to truly know how to give and receive love in the service of self and others.

Carole taught me this – she demonstrated this. Carole knew herself and was comfortable with her knowledge every day and in every way, and yet this was something that she was oblivious of. She was blind to her inner and outer beauty. She used to call our children her little butterflies. Carole was tuned to the frequency of love and joy that children communicate unknowingly to the people they interact with each day. Our children were her butterflies because they were completely unaware of the love and happiness they radiated. Carole is my butterfly of all seasons.

One of Mother Nature's most spectacular exhibits of evolution in my world of ideals is the journey of the butterfly. A peaceful advocate of essential and perfectly timed transformation, the butterfly cannot see itself as we see it through human eyes. It sees the fragile world in which we live using the ultraviolet spectrum of light. Perhaps this spectrum holds the key to the secrets bestowed beyond the universe of the mind. A butterfly never knows of its own beauty as we see it flying freely, nature's poetic resonance of ourselves. The inner butterfly of Carole's human nature was her inner beauty concealed in the secret chamber of her heart, waiting for the emotion-sensitive moment of release.

To release our inner butterfly is to bare our soul unconditionally from the inside out – from within and so without condition. Perhaps many of us never do this for fear of being hurt or because we've been hurt too many times before and so instinctively let fear become a protective mechanism. When falsely everything appears real, we find the fault that distorts our own heart's choices.

On the day that Carole and I first talked in our office, I think we must have abandoned any fears associated with life and love and so started to know love in a more powerful and intuitive form. Perhaps we laid bare our souls on that magical day and let them flirt at a frequency only understood by the butterflies we held for each other in the womb of our emotions. That was the moment I sensed we were soulmates.

If our soul is the butterfly of love, then we are each the source of unconditional love waiting patiently on the wings of our own human nature to fly. Is it coincidence that when we meet someone we are attracted to we say we get a feeling of butterflies? When we flirt with each other, our eyes naturally reveal external signals, fluttering messages of semaphore and metaphor that we like what we feel and we feel what we see. Perhaps this sensation is derived from the energies of two souls who play for a lifetime of moments in the theatre of their own ultraviolet dreams. Roses are red and violets are blue.

I love the romantic notion that the enchantment of our inner butterflies is itself the chemical intoxication of every sense that unlocks our sensitivity to feel the alchemy of love in every cell of our body. Is this same alchemy true and deep under the full draw of Cupid's bow and the magic of Puck's mystical flower of his master's thoughts? I like to think it to be. 'Tis the stimuli of dreams of the heart that makes love happen.

One of the hardest things about losing my soulmate is acknowledging the void that appears silently out of nowhere when I least expect it. It shows up and somehow I cope – I carry on, I smile, I cry, but I always cope. This is what I do, what we all do. We do whatever it takes wherever it takes us to get through these moments.

I catch my own reflection sometimes and she's missing. The reflection of a memory is tattooed feather-like across the back of a beautiful life that vibrates my soul in flutter and flight of spine-tingling magic. My void is entwined within a ring, a silver necklace, a photograph, a paper napkin, an unbalanced wedding cake, the first dance and the last one. It's in all the words of all the songs, all night long. It's a smell, a taste, a place, her favourite flowers, the sound of children at play, the empty passenger seat, and the absence of her hand to hold. It's her footprint in the sand. It's her minty breath on my face as she falls deeply to sleep nose–to-cheek in the arms that long to hold her just one more time until the end of time. It's in our traditions and anniversaries, laughing in the rain, feeding ducks, Easter-egg hunts and birthday's presence. Christmas shopping, mealtimes, a missed goodnight and the assurance of her goodnight kiss. It's physical. It's everywhere, and it aches like no other.

There's an emotional intensity that keeps me grounded and deeply honest within when all without has potential for chaos. To feel is to see the invisibility of pain that becomes an ache as it flies through a cranial brochure of a beautiful past and a love most kind. Memory is the gift that lasts forever; to truly remember is to think and to think is to be. I close my eyes sometimes and drift peacefully into a lofty space of colourful silence, of imagery and intuition that goes round and round and never ends.

When I think about love in a *revolving* world, I see circles and the word *lover*. Circles conjure a picture of completeness, of motion and infinity. For me, this manifests itself in the energy of earth and the planets, the skyward rotation of constellations and asterisms where perhaps stars and moons hide the keys that unlock the art in the heart of human kindness. A mystical coincidence, perhaps, that the words *earth* and *heart* have the same letters, just rearranged. Look again, and you'll see *art* in *heart*, and then other words appear: *hear*, *tear, her.* Circles are present in the eternal cycles of nature, in the symbolic completeness of a wedding ring, in the rotating arms of a windmill, in the infinity of 8, in an unsolved problem, and in the spiralling tick-tock of the dandelion clock. Circles are the shape of the bubbles in which I found my rainbows past, present, and future.

A carousel revolves and wheels go round as we travel. We evolve as we grow through infancy, childhood, adolescence, adulthood, and finally into the relativity of age. This reminds me of Carole's instinctive like and dislike of the four seasons. She loved the freshness and vibrancy of spring as her magical time of birth and rebirth, growth and learning. Intuitively, as a mother, she wove this season's natural sensitivities into the tapestry of her life.

Summer was always a period of mixed emotions, a subtle precursor to heart-break as flowers bloomed and revealed their inner beauty only to wither in the heat at the end of a natural life cycle. She saw this as a milestone in human nature, when maybe adolescence awakened as innocence departed. A time when the carefully sown seed of Carole's love would one day provide her children with freedom of thought, expression, sensitivity, and flight. I know Carole secretly feared the days when she'd have to witness first-hand the unfolding of tiny wings that is the transformation of her children's inner butterflies. As a path is cleared, they fly now courageously into the late spring and early summer of their own lives in glowing testament of Carole's strength, her motherhood, and her love. To watch them fly on my own is heart-breaking, but I am ever grateful for the opportunity and challenge of tomorrow's presents today.

In my moments of void and difference, the inner butterfly that Carole helped me to cultivate teaches me that the children will learn to be seasoned navigators in time, becoming more aware of the beauty of the world held within without their Mummy. My heart tells me every day that if I ever question the beauty, purpose, and wonder of life, I will find the answers every time in the eyes of the children. As they adapt their intuitive guidance systems, they'll find the place where dreams come true over rainbows skies. This is the place where there is no matter, where all that matters is love.

Carole loved autumn and winter best of all the seasons. Autumn was Carole's path-clearer and nature's own janitor preparing for regeneration, the consolidation of year-on-year growth creating space for maturity and a spark or two of wisdom. Remembering our crunchy autumn walks with the children and the crisp chill of fresh air upon rosy cheek, runny nose, and frozen toes see-saws my emotions every time. Carole loved the fade of an orange and gold autumn into winter's barren but magical wonderland, incubated by blankets of fog, rain, and snow.

Snow was the element that lit up Carole on the inside until she glowed with excitement and playfulness. Snow defines perfectly the character of Carole's inner child. She made snow angels on the ground during every snowfall of our life together. She loved to do this with her children, as they did with her. Carole was mesmerised by what she called the 'divine beauty of snow' when it drifted from the heavens to find its resting place on the ground, only to quietly disappear and transform active imagery to memory. The real magic of snow is perhaps that each flake is unique but joins itself with others as one when the conditions of nature so invite. If snow ever fell under the darkness of night, Carole would leave the bedroom curtains open and position her head on freshly plumped pillow to view the white fairy-like flakes dancing in silhouette under street lights against the black velvet of night sky.

When it snows, I now find myself mesmerised in the same way and picture Carole in the happy element of her snowy wonderland, snuggled in duvet, trying so hard not to fall asleep through one of nature's softest and most beautiful phenomena. Like Carole, I've always been fascinated by snow, but now I look at snowfall in a slightly different way. Although it continues to be a magical and happy time for me, I no longer just think 'it's snowing.' Instead, I say 'it's knowing.' It's knowing that life has shared with me one of its softest, most beautiful and uniquely delicate snowflakes. Carole was the snowflake who floated with my soul and dances at the heart of my dreams.

These colder seasons were like her maternal protectors and the blankets to all things in her nature. Autumn and winter may have been her reflected view of pregnancy where the Earth Mother radiates unnoticed for a while as she nurtures, keeps safe, protects, and begins to understand love as the unconditional and unbreakable bond with all her children. Carole showed me how this felt through her eyes and our senses. I witnessed first-hand how her bond intensified to reach its greatest depth at the height of her challenges. I saw how the unique relationship between mother and child was cultivated intuitively and so naturally through the divinely beautiful intoxication of feminine love – the love that breathes life into life. In Carole's world, this love was a seed she planted, protected, and nourished to take root and be released to blossom in the image of her own mirror.

Winter has potential to become the season of my discontent – but only if I let it. Winter is a period of conclusion, of agelessness, perhaps the end of one moment and the continuation of another. Perhaps it's a place of reconciliation, of peace, of trust, knowledge, belief and love. The dying embers of a winter's incubation symbolise the flight of my phoenix, new beginnings, and adventure. It can be whatever I think it to be in mind in body. In the natural world, winter may be the harshest season, when nature decides the fate of plant and creature. To me, winter's arrival will always signal a new advent of inflection. It incubates the seasonal whisper of love's ethereal echo, it animates the memory of her kiss and makes magic the diamond sparkle of every festive fairy light. Opportunity and challenge are the presents I open lovingly every morning upon waking. Removing their ribbons and bows teaches opportunity to remember, to celebrate and to learn from the strength and fragility of our personal history. Opportunity is to fly with the butterflies of my emotions around our wild flower meadow in a world of exquisite ultraviolet dreams. My challenge is to look honestly into the transformational mirror of my own nature and seek love in her most vulnerable, abundant and definitively beautiful form. In every mirror shines the self-compassion to evolve, to ignite, and harmonise the inner and outer worlds that coexist to define love at the heart of our collective, kind and loving nature. Carole showed me all that was her nature and now her love is teaching me to fly.

As I navigate a world of difference, I've found a place to be at peace with my emotions. My mirror of life shows me every day that this place is as I think it to be. This is a place that will never be the same and yet nothing has changed. It's a place within my heart where all is well and a well of memories incubate and keep safe a life of loves. This is a place where every moment is a lifetime and every life a moment of love in time. In this place, I realise love has no boundary and love only knows love.

May we all find happiness and love in our own place of dreams, rainbows and butterflies. In every moment embrace love, feel love and be open to love and see as you are intended to be seen.

Always with love, always three kisses: x x x.

X X
I am not who but how and when,
I am not tell but show and do,
I am not life or death,
I am your teacher,
I am love,
I am

X

For The Children

There is no such thing as coincidence.

There is only love.

I Love you

X

Unconditionally

For the girl with a garden of flowers, a heart of butterflies, soft of tear and sparkle smile. Shine bright like a diamond with rainbows of love in dreams of happiness forever a moment to be, to see, to feel, to blossom and to fly on the wings of love.

x

Love only knows love,

x

I love you

x

'Tis the stimuli of the dreams of our hearts
that make love happen.